What people are saying

"Here at Citibank we use the Quick Course® co[...] 'just-in-time' job aids—the books are great f[...] tutorials and training. Quick Course® books provide very clear instruction and easy reference."

Bill Moreno, Development Manager
Citibank
San Francisco, CA

"At Geometric Results, much of our work is PC related and we need training tools that can quickly and effectively improve the PC skills of our people. Early this year we began using your materials in our internal PC training curriculum and the results have been outstanding. Both participants and instructors like the books and the measured learning outcomes have been very favorable."

Roger Hill, Instructional Systems Designer
Geometric Results Incorporated
Southfield, MI

"The concise and well organized text features numbered instructions, screen shots, and useful quick reference pointers, and tips…[This] affordable text is very helpful for educators who wish to build proficiency."

Computer Literacy column
Curriculum Administrator Magazine
Stamford, CT

"I have purchased five other books on this subject that I've probably paid more than $60 for, and your [Quick Course®] book taught me more than those five books combined!"

Emory Majors
Searcy, AR

"I would like you to know how much I enjoy the Quick Course® books I have received from you. The directions are clear and easy to follow with attention paid to every detail of the particular lesson."

Betty Weinkauf, Retired Senior
Mission, TX

QUICK COURSE®

in

MICROSOFT®

OUTLOOK™
98

ONLINE PRESS INC.

Microsoft® *Press*

PUBLISHED BY
Microsoft Press
A Division of Microsoft Corporation
One Microsoft Way
Redmond, WA 98052-6399

Library of Congress Cataloging-in-Publication Data

Quick Course in Microsoft Outlook 98 / Online Press Inc.
     p.   cm.
   Includes index.
   ISBN 1-57231-846-5
   1. Microsoft Outlook.   2. Time management - - Computer programs.
  3. Personal information management - - Computer programs
  4. Electronic mail systems.   I. Online Press Inc.
  HD69.T54Q85   1998
  005.369 - - dc21   98-12107
                                            CIP

Printed and bound in the United States of America.

2 3 4 5 6 7 8 9 WCWC 3 2 1 0 9 8

Distributed to the book trade in Canada by Macmillan of Canada, a division of Canada Publishing Corporation.

A CIP record for this book is available from the British Library.

Microsoft Press books are available through booksellers and distributors worldwide. For further information about international editions, contact your local Microsoft Corporation office, or contact Microsoft Press International directly at fax (425) 936-7329. Visit our Web site at mspress.microsoft.com.

A Quick Course® Education/Training Edition for this title is published by Online Press Inc. For information about supplementary workbooks, contact Online Press Inc. at 14320 NE 21st St., Suite 18, Bellevue, WA, 98007, USA, 1-800-854-3344.

Authors: Christina Dudley and Joyce Cox of Online Press Inc., Bellevue, Washington
Acquisitions Editor: Susanne M. Forderer
Project Editor: Maureen Williams Zimmerman

From the publisher

"I love these books!"

I can't tell you the number of times people have said those exact words to me about our new Quick Course® software training book series. And when I ask them what makes the books so special, this is what they say:

- **They're short and approachable, but they give you hours worth of good information.**

  Written for busy people with limited time, most Quick Course books are designed to be completed in 15 to 40 hours. Because Quick Course books are usually divided into two parts—Learning the Basics and Building Proficiency—users can selectively choose the chapters that meet their needs and complete them as time allows.

- **They're relevant and fun, and they assume you're no dummy.**

  Written in an easy-to-follow, step-by-step format, Quick Course books offer stream-lined instruction for the new user in the form of no-nonsense, to-the-point tutorials and learning exercises. Each book provides a logical sequence of instructions for creating useful business documents—the same documents people use on the job. People can either follow along directly or substitute their own information and customize the documents. After finishing a book, users have a valuable "library" of documents they can continually recycle and update with new information.

- **They're direct and to the point, and they're a lot more than just pretty pictures.**

  Training-oriented rather than feature-oriented, Quick Course books don't cover the things you don't really need to know to do useful work. They offer easy-to-follow, step-by-step instructions; lots of screen shots for checking work in progress; quick-reference pointers for fast, easy lookup and review; and useful tips offering additional information on topics being discussed.

- **They're a rolled-into-one-book solution, and they meet a variety of training needs.**

  Designed with instructional flexibility in mind, Quick Course books can be used both for self-training and as the basis for weeklong courses, two-day seminars, and all-day workshops. They can be adapted to meet a variety of training needs, including classroom instruction, take-away practice exercises, and self-paced learning.

Microsoft Press is very excited about bringing you this extraordinary series. But you must be the judge. I hope you'll give these books a try. And maybe the next time I see you, you too will say, "Hey, Jim! I love these books!"

Jim Brown, Publisher
Microsoft Press

Content overview

Content details

1

Introducing Outlook 98

We introduce the Outlook window and give you an overview of what you can do with Outlook's various components. Then we show you how to use the Notes component to jot down reminders, while demonstrating a few of the organizing techniques that are available with all the components.

Create electronic notes
to remind yourself of
important items

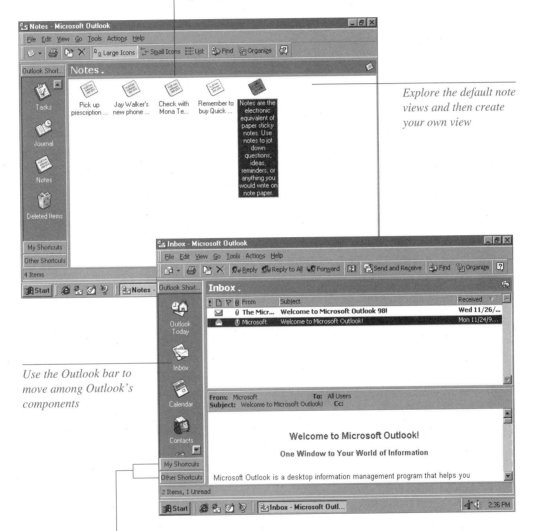

Explore the default note
views and then create
your own view

Use the Outlook bar to
move among Outlook's
components

Use these buttons to display
other groups of icons, and
then add icons of your own

Until recently, it was not uncommon for people to keep track of their appointments, tasks, and other information either in their heads or on various pieces of paper. It's not surprising that things were forgotten or notes were lost, because pieces of paper could easily get buried under paperwork on a desk or could accidentally be moved to the recycling bin. More organized people maintained their information in day-planners, expense recorders, and address books, and either carried several small books around with them or kept everything in a hefty all-in-one organizer.

With the integration of the computer into everyday office life, storing vital business and personal information electronically is a natural step. Although information-management software has been around for some time, in the past programs may have handled some types of information but not others, or may have done a poor job of sharing the information with other programs. Microsoft Outlook, which was introduced with Microsoft Office 97, signaled a breakthrough in the integration of common information-management tasks with productivity programs. The latest version, Outlook 98, continues the trend toward tight integration and cross-program accessibility of business and personal information.

What Is Outlook?

We use Outlook to manage the information that we might record in an assortment of address books, appointment books, and notebooks, as well as to handle e-mail. Outlook includes the following components, all of which can be easily customized to fit your needs or preferred methods of organization:

Outlook components

- **Outlook Today.** Provides a handy overview of what's on our plate today. Included are appointments from our calendar and tasks from our to-do list, the number of new e-mail messages we've received, and a handy place to look up someone in our contacts list.

- **Inbox.** Keeps track of all our e-mail (and electronic faxes). If we are working on a network that uses Microsoft Exchange Server, we can communicate with coworkers via our company's e-mail system, and if we have an Internet account, any Internet e-mail we receive will also show up in our Inbox.

- **Calendar.** Records appointments, including those that occur on a regular basis, such as once a month. We can set Calendar to remind us as an appointment's time approaches. If we are using Microsoft Exchange Server, we can also use this component to schedule meetings with coworkers.

- **Contacts.** Functions as an address book but can store much more information. We can categorize our contacts and store them in different folders, and we can view information in a variety of formats.

- **Tasks.** Maintains a to-do list. To keep us on track, we can set Tasks to display reminders or sound alarms, and we can schedule time in Calendar for working on to-do list items.

- **Journal.** Automatically records computer activities, such as working on a document or sending an e-mail message. We can also create manual journal entries to track phone calls and other types of information.

- **Notes.** Creates reminders that replace hand-written notes. We can leave the reminders open on the desktop, organize them from within the Notes component, or move the information they contain to another Outlook component.

In this chapter, we discuss some Outlook basics by introducing you to the Notes component. We will get to know the Outlook window, learn how to create notes, and see how to customize our view of the window's contents. Many of the techniques we demonstrate with Notes also apply to the other Outlook components, which we'll discuss in the remaining chapters. In this book, we focus on Outlook's most useful features—the ones most people will use most often and the ones more people would use if they knew how. By the time you finish this Quick Course book, you'll have a firm understanding of the components of Outlook, and you'll know enough to experiment on your own with the features we don't cover in detail.

Two Outlook flavors

There are some features of Outlook that are available only if you are working on a network that runs Microsoft Exchange Server. When Outlook is installed on your computer, the setup program detects whether the computer is connected to a network and whether it has a modem, and configures Outlook for Corporate Support on networked computers or Internet Support on stand-alone computers. If the setup program cannot determine how you are most likely to use Outlook, it may display a dialog box or two requesting clarification.

The Microsoft Outlook icon

Automatic Outlook start-up

To have Outlook start automatically every time you turn on your computer, you can add an Outlook shortcut to your StartUp menu. Right-click a blank area of the taskbar and choose Properties from the object menu. When the Taskbar Properties dialog box appears, click the Start Menu Programs tab, click the Add button to start the Create Shortcut Wizard, and then click the Browse button in the wizard's first dialog box. Navigate to the Microsoft Office subfolder of the Program Files folder, double-click Microsoft Outlook, and then click Next. In the wizard's second dialog box, select the StartUp subfolder of the Programs folder and click Next. Click Finish in the wizard's last dialog box. Click OK to close the Taskbar Properties dialog box. The next time you start Windows, Outlook will be ready and waiting for you.

Getting Started

We assume that Outlook has been installed on your computer either separately or as part of the Microsoft Office package. We also assume that you've worked with Microsoft Windows 95 (or later) or Microsoft Windows NT 4 (or later). If you are new to these versions of Windows, we recommend you take a look at a corresponding book in the Quick Course series, which will help you quickly come up to speed.

Let's take a look at Outlook now. Follow these steps:

1. On the Windows desktop, double-click the Microsoft Outlook icon to start the program. (You can also click the Start button, choose Programs from the Start menu, and then choose Microsoft Outlook from the Programs submenu.)

2. If Outlook displays a dialog box so that you can choose a profile, select your profile name if it is available, or click OK.

3. If Outlook displays a message box something like this one:

click Yes to set up Outlook as your default manager.

4. If necessary, close the Office Assistant. (We discuss the Office Assistant in more detail on page 29.)

5. If Outlook displays a dialog box about archiving files, click No. (We discuss archiving on page 130.)

6. Maximize the Outlook window, which should look something like the one shown at the top of the facing page.

Microsoft recommends that Outlook users set the screen resolution to 800 x 600 *dpi* (dots per inch). For legibility, we set our screen to 640 x 480 dpi. If you need to change your screen resolution, check the "resolution of screen" topic in Outlook's online help. (See page 28 for more information.)

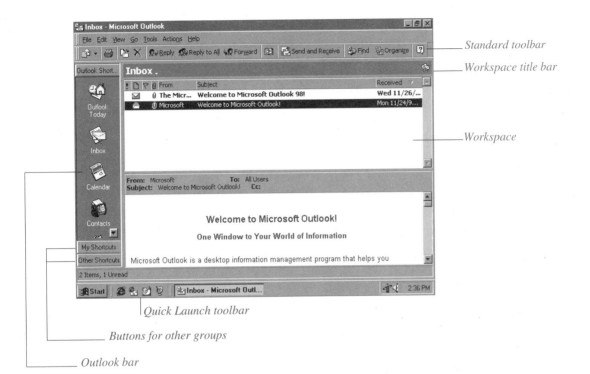

Standard toolbar

Workspace title bar

Workspace

Quick Launch toolbar

Buttons for other groups

Outlook bar

By default, Outlook opens with the Inbox component displayed. If your computer is set up to handle e-mail, either through your company network or through a modem and an Internet service provider (ISP), Outlook may fetch and display any new and existing e-mail messages. If your computer is not set up to handle e-mail, Inbox will be empty. (We discuss e-mail in more detail in Chapter 3.)

Like most Windows applications, a title bar, menu bar, and toolbar span the top of the Outlook window, and a status bar spans the bottom. Let's take a quick look at each of them:

- **Title bar.** Identifies the program. At its left end is the *Control menu* (represented by the envelope/clock icon), which provides commands for manipulating the application's window. At its right end are the *Minimize button* (the dash), which shrinks the application window to a button on the Windows taskbar; the *Restore button* (the overlapping frames), which decreases the size of the application window to its previous size; and the *Close button* (the X), which closes the window and exits the program. (If you are running Outlook as

Changing the default starting component

If you use a different Outlook component more often than Inbox, you can specify that Outlook display that component's window when the program starts. To change the default starting component, choose Options from the Tools menu and on the Other tab, click Advanced Options in the General section. Click the arrow to the right of the Startup In This Folder edit box and select the desired component. Then click OK twice. The next time you start Outlook, the program will open with the window of the component you selected displayed in the workspace.

part of Microsoft Office, you may see the *Office shortcut bar* sitting on top of the title bar.)

Choosing commands

- **Menu bar.** Provides access to commands for working with Outlook. The Outlook menus work the same as those of other Windows applications. To choose a command from a menu, first click the name of the menu in the menu bar. When the menu drops down, click the name of the command. To close a menu without choosing a command, click anywhere outside the menu.

On the menus, some command names are displayed in gray letters, indicating that we can't choose those commands at this time, and some command names have an arrowhead next to them, indicating that choosing the command will display a *submenu*. We choose a submenu command the same way we choose a regular command.

Some command names are followed by an ellipsis (...), indicating that we must supply more information in a *dialog box* before Outlook can carry out the command. We sometimes give the necessary information by typing in an *edit box*. At other times, we might select items in *list boxes* or click *check boxes* or *option buttons* to indicate our selections. We'll use many types of dialog boxes as we work our way through this book, and you'll see how easy they are to work with.

- **Standard toolbar.** Displays a row of buttons that quickly access the most commonly used menu commands. Outlook displays different buttons on this toolbar depending on the component we are working with. To avoid confusion, a feature called *ScreenTips* helps us determine the function of buttons that have no text labels. When we point to a button, a pop-up box appears with the button's name.

- **Status bar.** Displays messages and provides helpful information. (Currently, it displays how many items are listed in Inbox.)

Between the Standard toolbar and the status bar, the Outlook window is divided into *panes*. The vertical pane on the left, called the *Outlook bar*, displays one of three groups of icons.

The Office shortcut bar

The Office shortcut bar includes buttons for creating e-mail messages, appointments, tasks, contacts, journal entries, and new notes. These buttons come in handy when you are working in another program and suddenly remember an appointment you need to make or a message you want to send. If you use Outlook frequently, you may want to install the shortcut bar if it's not already available. Choose Settings and then Control Panel from the Start menu, double-click the Add/Remove Programs icon, select Microsoft Office in the Add/Remove list, and then click the Add/Remove button at the bottom of the Install/Uninstall tab. Insert the Office installation CD-ROM and click OK. In the Microsoft Office Setup dialog box, click the Add/Remove button, select the Office Tools option, and click Change Option. Click the Microsoft Office Shortcut Bar check box, click OK, and then click OK to proceed with the installation.

The current group, called Outlook Shortcuts, includes icons that represent the various Outlook components. Clicking the down arrow at the bottom of the group brings more icons into view. Clicking the My Shortcuts button at the bottom of the Outlook bar opens that group and displays icons related to e-mail. Clicking the Other Shortcuts button displays icons for My Computer as well as other folders that enable you to quickly find files or jump to specific Web sites.

The large pane on the right, called the *workspace*, displays the contents of the icon selected in the Outlook bar.

In the case of Inbox, the workspace is further divided into a *summary pane*, which displays information about the messages in Inbox, and a *preview pane*, which displays the text of the message selected in the summary pane. (For more information about displaying and reading e-mail messages, see page 65.) Let's explore to see exactly how the Outlook window works:

1. Click various icons on the Outlook bar to jump from one component to another, and then redisplay Inbox in the workspace.

2. Now click the My Shortcuts button at the bottom of the Outlook bar to display that group of icons, as shown here:

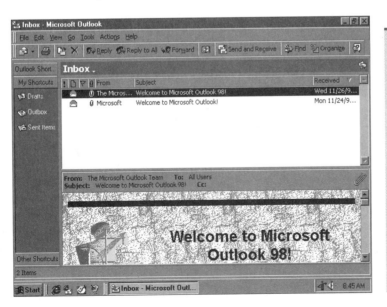

Streamlining the Outlook bar

When a group contains more icons than will fit on the Outlook bar, you may want to view them all without having to use the arrows. Simply change the icon size by right-clicking a blank area of the Outlook bar and choosing Small Icons from the object menu. If you want to switch back to large icons, right-click and choose Large Icons. For more information about customizing the Outlook bar, see page 26.

3. Click the Other Shortcuts button at the bottom of the Outlook bar to display the icons shown here. (Don't worry if you don't have all these icons. Outlook's display varies depending on whether you are using Outlook on a stand-alone computer or a networked computer.)

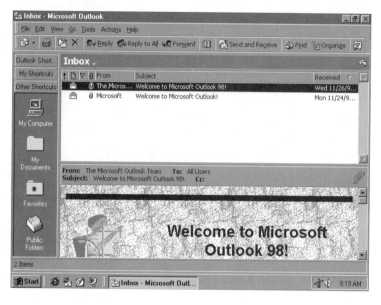

4. To return to the Outlook Shortcuts group, click the Outlook Shortcuts button at the top of the bar.

5. Now click the down arrow at the bottom of the bar a few times until you see the Notes icon.

The Notes icon

6. Click the Notes icon. Because you haven't yet created any notes, the workspace is empty. But notice that the buttons on the Standard toolbar have changed, and the workspace title bar and the button on the taskbar indicate that the Notes component is now active.

As we mentioned earlier, the Notes component allows us to jot down any tidbits of information we want to keep handy. The main advantage of keeping notes in Outlook instead of on pieces of paper is that we can easily use the information contained in the note with a different Outlook component.

Creating Notes

The best way to see how the Notes component of Outlook works is to start creating some notes. Suppose we want to remind ourselves to purchase another book in the Quick Course series. Follow these steps:

The New Note button

1. With the Notes window displayed, click the New Note button on the Standard toolbar. Outlook displays a small yellow box, similar to the "sticky" notes used in most offices:

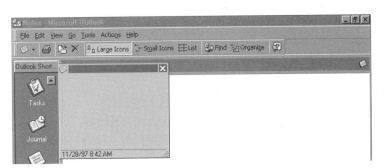

The note box has an icon in the top left corner that you can click to display a menu of commands related to the note, and a Close button (the X) in the top right corner. At the bottom of the note box is the date and time the note was created.

2. With the insertion point blinking in the blank note box, type *Remember to buy Quick Course in Office.*

3. Outlook automatically saves the note as soon as you close it, so simply click the Close button.

4. Now create a few more notes by clicking the New Note button on the Standard toolbar and typing the ones listed below. (Be sure to click the Close button when you finish one note and click the New Note button to start a new one.)

   Check with Mona Terry about new account

   Jay Walker's new phone number: 206-555-1458

   Pick up prescription at drug store

5. When you finish the last note, click its Close button. Your screen now looks like the one shown on the following page.

Other ways to create notes

To create a note while you are working in another Outlook component, click the arrow to the right of the New Item button on the toolbar and select Note, or choose New and then Note from the File menu. If you are using Microsoft Office, you can create a note when you don't have Outlook open by clicking the New Note button on the Office shortcut bar. (If you haven't yet installed the Office shortcut bar, see the tip on page 8.)

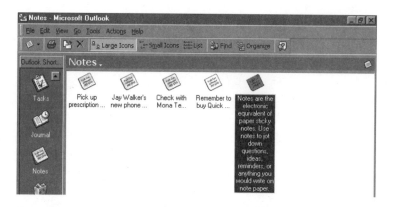

Notes displays the entire text of the selected note and the first few words of all the others. To select a note, simply click it.

Editing and Organizing Notes

Suppose we want to edit a note we have created. Or suppose we want to change its color to make it stand out or organize the notes into categories. Let's experiment:

1. Double-click the Quick Course book reminder, select the word *Office*, and type *Windows*.

2. Change the color of the note from yellow to green by clicking the icon in the top left corner of the note box and choosing Color and Green from the menu. The note box changes color.

3. You don't want this personal note to get buried among your business-related notes, so click the icon again and choose Categories from the Notes menu to display this dialog box:

Saving notes

Because notes are constantly saved, you can open a note, make a change, and then click anywhere outside the note to save the change. If you want to save a note for use in another program, open the note, click the icon in the top left corner, choose Save As from the menu, and assign a name and storage location as you would with any other file. By default, Outlook saves the note as a Rich Text Format (RTF) file. To select a different format, click the arrow to the right of the Save As Type box and make your selection.

4. Click the Personal check box in the Available Categories list and click OK. Although nothing appears to happen, Notes now stores this note in the personal category, as you will see when we discuss the different Notes views on page 17.

5. Save and close the note by clicking its Close button.

6. Double-click the Mona Terry note, repeat steps 3 and 4 to assign the note to the business category, and close the note.

7. Double-click the prescription note, assign it to the personal category, change its color to green, and close it.

8. Now double-click the Jay Walker note and assign it to the business category, but don't close the note box.

9. Move the mouse pointer to the bottom right corner of the box, and, when the pointer changes to a double-headed arrow, hold down the mouse button and drag diagonally toward the top left corner. Release the mouse button when the box is just big enough to display its text, as shown here:

Sizing notes

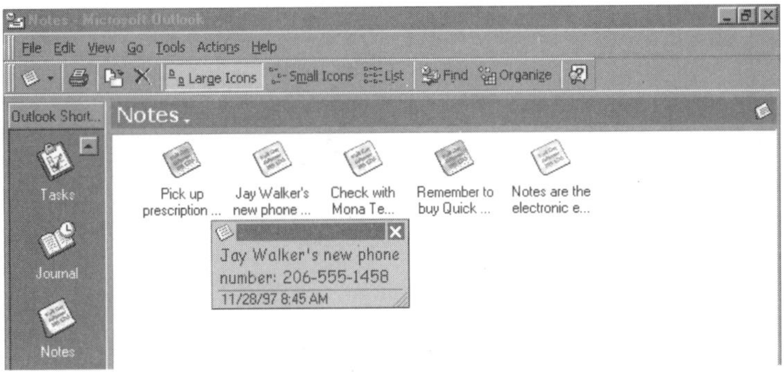

The note box remains this size unless you change it again.

10. Click the note's Close button to save your changes and to close the box.

Moving Notes

You may be wondering why the Notes feature is so great if we can't see the notes when we move to another Outlook component or to a different application. Fortunately, we can move our notes onto the desktop and display them there no matter what application we are working with. We can also move the contents of the note to another Outlook component.

Moving a Note to the Desktop

Suppose the Mona Terry note is important, and we want to be able to see it while we work on other things, just so we won't forget it. Follow these steps to make the note accessible even if Outlook is not running:

1. With Notes displayed on your screen, double-click the Mona Terry note to open it in its box.

2. Resize the box so that it is just large enough to display its text.

3. Minimize Outlook by clicking the Minimize button at the right end of the title bar. The active note now appears on the desktop, as shown here:

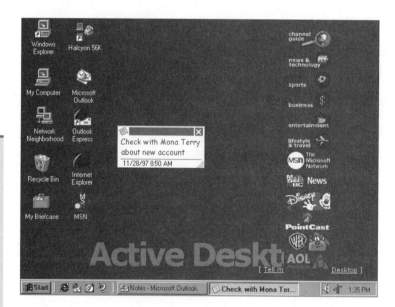

Changing note defaults

To change the Notes default color, choose Options from the Tools menu. Click the Preferences tab and click the Note Options button. Change the note color by clicking the arrow to the right of the Color box and making a selection. You can change the default note-box size by clicking the arrow to the right of the Size box and making a selection. To change the default font for notes, click the Font button to display the Font dialog box, make your changes, and then click OK. To implement your changes, click OK twice.

4. Move the note box to the bottom of the screen by pointing to its title bar, holding down the left mouse button, and dragging to the desired location. When the box is where you want it, release the mouse button.

5. Now double-click the My Computer icon and maximize the My Computer window. The note seems to disappear, but it has actually been minimized on the taskbar.

Minimizing a note

6. Point to the Check with Mona ... button on the taskbar. Windows displays a pop-up box containing the text of the note, as shown here:

Displaying a note's text

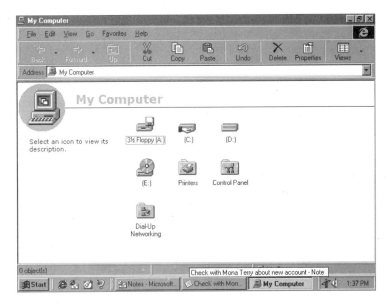

If the note were longer, only the first several words would be displayed.

7. To display the note box, simply click the button on the taskbar. An insertion point is blinking in the note box, ready for you to make any changes.

Displaying a note box

8. Click the note's Close button and then close My Computer.

9. Click the Notes button on the taskbar to redisplay the Outlook window.

Moving a Note to a Different Outlook Component

If we want to move the text of a note to another Outlook component, we simply select the note in the Notes workspace and drag it to the appropriate Outlook component icon. For example, suppose we want to convert the prescription note into a task on our to-do list. Follow these steps:

1. Click the prescription note once to select it, point to it, hold down the left mouse button, and drag the note to the Tasks icon on the Outlook bar.

2. When the shadowed box attached to the pointer is positioned over the Tasks icon, release the mouse button. Outlook displays this window, with the text of the note displayed in the Subject edit box:

Attaching a note to another Outlook item

Sometimes you may want a note to appear as an attachment inside another Outlook item. For example, you might want to write the instructions for getting to a business conference as a note and then attach the instructions to an appointment in your calendar. To attach a note to another Outlook item, open the component and the item and choose Item from the Insert menu. In the Insert Item dialog box, click the Notes folder to display its contents and then select the appropriate note from the Items list at the bottom of the dialog box. Check that the Attachment option is selected in the Insert As section and then click OK. Now the note is embedded in the Outlook item. To open the note, simply double-click it.

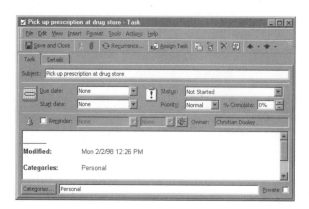

Notice the chevrons at the right end of the toolbar, indicating that this window has more buttons available than are visible at this window's size. Maximize the window to view the remaining buttons.

3. We discuss the Tasks component in Chapter 5, so for now click the window's Close button and click No in the message box to close the window without saving the changes.

As you read the remaining chapters of this book, bear in mind that you can easily move the contents of a note to another Outlook component to get you started in creating a new contact, appointment, or e-mail message. Very handy!

Deleting Notes

When a note is no longer useful, we will want to delete it to keep it from hogging space in the Notes workspace and on our hard drive. Follow these steps to delete the prescription note:

1. With the Notes window displayed, click the prescription note once to select it.

2. Click the Delete button on the Standard toolbar. The note instantly disappears.

The Delete button

3. Suppose you decide you don't want to delete this note after all. You haven't made any other editing changes, so choose Undo Delete from the Edit menu to redisplay the note.

4. Choose Redo Delete from the Edit menu to delete the note again.

5. Next, delete the default note (*Notes are the electronic e...*).

Switching Views

We are not limited to the large icon view that Outlook uses to display our notes. One of the main benefits of Outlook is that the program is easily customizable to our needs. Let's explore some of the different ways we can view notes, bearing in mind that we can also look at items in the other Outlook components in similar ways:

1. Click first the Small Icons button and then the List button on the toolbar to see what those icon views look like.

2. Click the Large Icons button to redisplay the original view.

   Perhaps none of these icon views quite fits the bill. Let's look at some of the table views Outlook has to offer:

1. Choose Current View and then Notes List from the View menu to display the notes in the table view shown on the following page.

Retrieving deleted items

If you decide later that you want to retrieve a note (or another Outlook item), you can display the contents of the Deleted Items folder by clicking its icon on the Outlook bar. Select the note you want to retrieve and drag it to the Notes icon. When you display Notes in the workspace, the retrieved note will be back in its place.

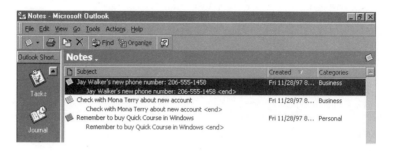

As you can see, Outlook displays information about the notes in Icon, Subject, Created, and Categories fields. The Icon field displays a note icon of the appropriate color, and the Subject field displays the first few lines of the note (using an ellipsis if the entire text is too long to fit in the alloted space). The Created field displays the date and time the note was created, and the Categories field displays the category the note is assigned to, if any.

Sizing fields

2. Point to the border between the Subject and Created field headers, and when you see the mouse pointer change to a double-headed arrow, drag to the left. Release the mouse button when the Subject field is just wide enough to display the text of the three notes. (Notice that the Created and Categories fields expand so that you can read more of their information.)

3. Choose Current View and then By Category from the View menu. The Notes window now looks like this:

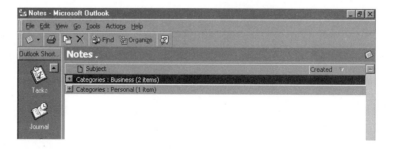

The notes are now grouped by the category to which you assigned them, using the Icon, Subject, and Created fields.

4. To display a list of the notes in a category, click the category's plus sign. For example, the window looks like this after you expand both categories:

Expanding categories

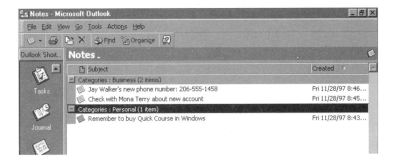

5. To collapse the categories again, simply click each category's minus sign.

Contracting categories

6. Now select the By Color view from the Current View submenu to display a window in which the notes are grouped by color.

7. Finally, select the Last Seven Days view from the Current View submenu to display only notes created in the last seven days. (In this case, all three notes were created within the last seven days, so this option looks similar to Notes List view.)

Creating Your Own View

Suppose none of Outlook's views organizes our notes exactly the way we want them. We don't have to settle for the closest match because, with Outlook, we can create our own view. Here's how to modify an existing view to create a new one that suits us:

1. Switch to the By Color view and choose Current View and then Customize Current View from the View menu to display the dialog box shown on the next page.

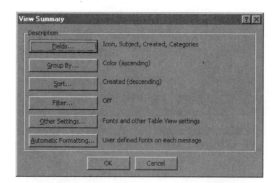

Sorting (grouping) notes ──────▶ **2.** Click the Group By button to display this dialog box:

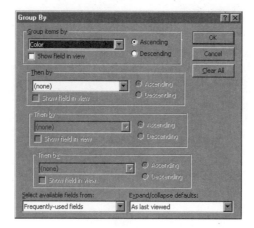

You can select up to four grouping levels for your notes. By default, the Group Items By edit box uses the selected view as the first grouping order (in this case, Color). You can then select either Ascending (A to Z or lowest to highest digit) or Descending (Z to A or highest to lowest digit) to determine how that grouping should be sorted.

3. For this example, leave the default Ascending option in the Group Items By section selected.

4. Click the arrow to the right of the first Then By edit box and select Created. Check that the Descending option next to the edit box is selected and then click OK in both dialog boxes. Outlook sorts the notes by color and displays the colors. Within each color, Outlook sorts by creation date and time, with the most recent note in each color category first.

5. Click the plus sign next to each color category.

6. Next, click the plus sign next to each Created subcategory to display the details of each note, as shown here:

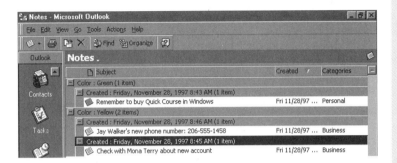

Grouping items

To quickly group items in any table view, you can use the Group By This Field command. When you right-click a field header in a table view and choose this command from the object menu, Outlook displays a Group By box above the table in the workspace. To group by a particular field, simply drag the field's header to the Group By box. Outlook instantly sorts the items in the table by that field and removes the field's information from the table. To group by more than one field using the Group By box, drag another field's header to the box and release the mouse button when the red double-headed arrow appears to the right of the first field header. If you want this new field to be the first group-by field, drag the field header to the left of the current first field. To fine-tune any grouping, double-click an empty area of the box to display the Group By dialog box. To remove a grouping field entirely, drag the field header anywhere outside the Group By box and release the mouse button when Outlook displays a large black X over the column heading. To return a field header and its information to the table, drag the field header over to the table's header row, releasing the header when it is positioned where you want it. To close the Group By box, right-click a field header in the table and choose Group By Box from the object menu.

7. Repeat steps 1 and 2 to open the Group By dialog box again, select (None) from the first Then By edit box, and click OK twice to redisplay the notes sorted by color only.

If we want an even more flexible way of changing views or creating new ones, we can use the Define Views dialog box. Follow these steps:

1. Choose Current View and then Define Views from the View menu to display this dialog box:

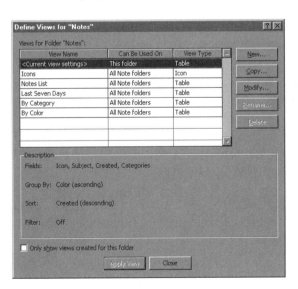

At the top of the dialog box, Outlook displays a list of the available views (in this case, the current view and the five default Notes views). Information about the view selected in the list appears in the Description section. You can create a new view from scratch by clicking the New button, copy a view (so that you can rename it and modify it to create a new view) by clicking the Copy button, and modify an existing view by clicking the Modify button.

Copying a view to create a new one

2. With Current View Settings selected, click the Copy button to display this dialog box:

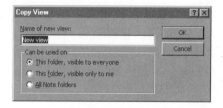

3. Type *My View* in the Name Of New View edit box and click OK to open the View Summary dialog box shown on page 20.

4. Next, click the Fields button to display this dialog box:

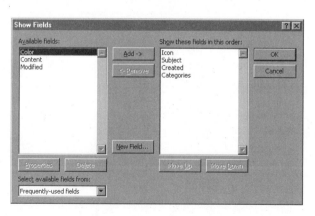

The available fields

The fields listed in the Available Fields box are determined by the setting in the Select Available Fields From edit box. You might want to select various options from this drop-down list to see the range of fields that can be added to custom table views.

5. The Icon field isn't very useful, so select it in the Show These Fields In This Order box and click the Remove button.

6. Click Modified in the Available Fields box and click the Add button to add a field that records when the note was last edited.

7. To move the Modified field to the bottom of the list, click the Move Down button twice. Then click OK to return to the View Summary dialog box.

Specifying field order

Our custom view now has the fields we want, but suppose we'd like to add gridlines to the table. Follow these steps:

1. Click the Other Settings button to display this dialog box:

Changing the formatting of a custom view

Other Settings

Column headings
[Font...] [8 pt. Tahoma] ☑ Automatic column sizing
[OK]
[Cancel]

Rows
[Font...] [8 pt. Tahoma] ☐ Allow in-cell editing
☐ Show "new item" row

AutoPreview
[Font...] [8 pt. Tahoma] ○ Preview all items
○ Preview unread items
◉ No AutoPreview

Grid lines
Grid line style: [No grid lines ▼] Preview: [   ]
Grid line color: [   ] ☑ Shade group headings

Preview Pane
☐ Show Preview Pane
☐ Hide header information

You can use the first few sections of this dialog box to change the font for various parts of the note.

2. Click the arrow to the right of the Grid Line Style box in the Grid Lines section and select Solid.

3. Click the arrow to the right of the Grid Line Color box and select a color you feel is appropriate. Then click OK twice to close first the Other Settings dialog box and then the View Summary dialog box.

4. Click Close to close the Define Views dialog box and to create the new view.

5. Choose Current View and then My View from the View menu and if necessary, expand the categories. The Notes workspace displays solid colored gridlines between entries, includes a Modified field at the end of the table, and no longer includes an Icon field, as shown on the next page.

Moving fields manually

To move fields manually in any table view, simply point to the header of the field you want to move, hold down the left mouse button, and drag the header to the desired location. Outlook displays a red arrow to show where the column will move when you release the mouse button. You can move fields this way in any Outlook component.

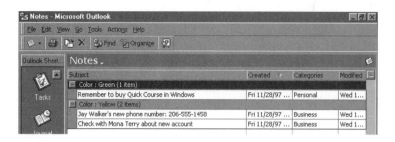

If we decide we no longer need a custom view, we can delete it. Follow these steps:

1. Switch to the By Color view.

Deleting a custom view

2. Choose Current View and then Define Views from the View menu to display the dialog box shown earlier on page 21.

3. Select My View from the Views list and click the Delete button. Click OK to confirm the deletion, and then click Close.

Customizing the Outlook Window

So far we have looked at ways to customize our view of information in the workspace. But we can also modify parts of the Outlook window to get a better view of our information and to keep our other resources within easy reach. While you are still learning to use Outlook, you may want to stick with the default setup to keep things simple, but as you get more familiar with the program, you might want to start experimenting with some of the capabilities we'll quickly cover in this section until you find the configuration that best suits the way you work.

Increasing the Size of the Workspace

No matter how we change the view of our information in the workspace, we may find that it is simply too small to show everything we need. The simple solution is to reclaim space taken up by some of the Outlook window's other elements. Follow these steps:

1. Choose Status Bar from the View menu to turn off the bar at the bottom of the window.

The Organize button

You can use the Organize button as another method for organizing Outlook items and changing views. When you click the Organize button on the Standard toolbar, Outlook opens a pane in the top half of the workspace to help streamline the organization process. With the Using Folders option selected, you can tell Outlook to move items to other folders or make a rule to move all similar items created in the future by a certain person to a particular folder. You can simply click New Folder to create a new folder or click Rules Wizard to set up more complex organization rules. If you click Using Views, you can select a different view or customize the current view. To close the Organize pane, either click its Close button or click the Organize button again to toggle it off.

2. Point to the right border of the Outlook bar and drag to the left as far as you can.

3. Now right-click the Outlook bar and choose Hide Outlook Bar from the object menu. Your screen now looks like this:

Hiding the Outlook bar

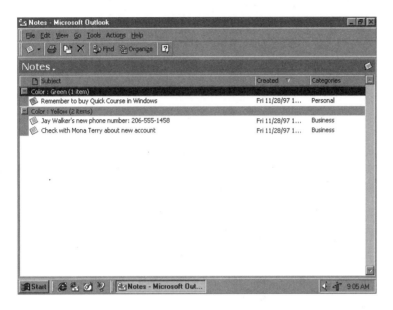

To give yourself even more room, you can hide the Windows taskbar. To see how, follow the instructions on page 137.

Well, that's all well and good, but how do we move from one Outlook component to another now? Try this:

1. Click the down arrow to the right of the word *Notes* in the workspace title bar to display a list of all the available destinations, and click Inbox to display its contents in the expanded workspace.

Moving among Outlook components

2. Click the down arrow to the right of *Inbox* and then click Notes to redisplay its contents.

3. Click the down arrow and then click the push pin in the title bar of the list box to keep the list open, as shown on the following page.

The Push Pin icon

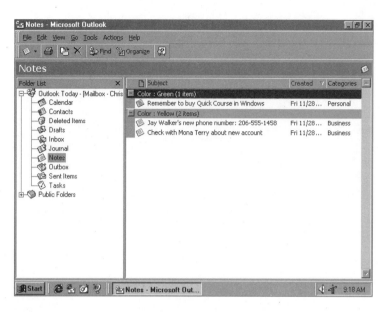

4. To close the list, you can click the Close button in its title bar, but here's another way. Choose Folder List from the View menu to deselect it. (You can also choose this toggle command to display the list.)

5. Choose Outlook Bar from the View menu to turn the bar back on, and then restore its original size by dragging its right border to the right. Then redisplay the status bar.

The Advanced toolbar

If you want certain menu commands more readily available, you may want to explore the Advanced toolbar. To display this toolbar, choose Toolbars and then Advanced from the View menu. (You can also right-click the Standard toolbar and then choose Advanced from the object menu.) Most of the buttons on the Advanced toolbar deal with various view options. For example, you can click the arrow to the right of the Current View box to select a different view. You can also display the folder list by clicking its button.

Another way of moving around when we have turned off the Outlook bar is to choose commands from the Go menu. We can move directly to Outlook Today, Inbox, Calendar, Contacts, and Tasks, and we can move to any other destination by choosing Go To Folder to display a dialog box similar to the folder list. If we primarily use only two of Outlook's components, we can flip between them by choosing the Back and Forward commands. You might want to check out this menu on your own before moving on.

Customizing the Outlook Bar

When you first start working with Outlook, you may think of it as just a personal information and e-mail manager. But Outlook is flexible enough to function as the interface through which we can initiate many of the other tasks we need to perform throughout the day. By adding shortcuts for folders to the Outlook bar, we can quickly open documents without ever having to close Outlook.

In this section, we briefly look at ways to add these shortcuts and otherwise modify the Outlook bar. For demonstration purposes, suppose we keep all our current work in a Projects folder on our hard drive and we want to keep this folder close at hand so that we can easily open any of its documents. Follow these steps to create the folder:

1. Click the Other Shortcuts button at the bottom of the Outlook bar, and then click the My Computer icon to display its contents in the workspace.

Creating a new folder

2. Double-click the icon for your hard drive to display its contents, and choose New and then Folder from the File menu.

3. Type *Projects* as the name of the new folder and press Enter.

Now we'll show you how to add a shortcut for the folder to the Other Shortcuts group:

1. Select the Projects folder and drag it to the Other Shortcuts group of the Outlook bar, positioning it below the Favorites folder so that you see a black bar between Favorites and Public Folders. Your screen looks like this:

Adding shortcuts to the Outlook bar

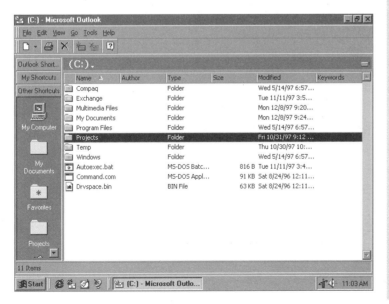

Dragging to another group

To drag folders and files from one group to another, display the item you want to move. Select it and then drag it to the appropriate group button on the Outlook bar. Pause until Outlook displays the group's contents in the Outlook bar. Position the pointer in the desired location. (Outlook will display a black bar between items to show where the item you are moving will appear.) If you drag a folder to a different group, Outlook's default action is to move it. (You can copy it by holding down the Ctrl key.) Files, on the other hand, are copied by default.

To work on a document stored in the Projects folder, we can simply click Projects in the Outlook bar to display its contents in the workspace, and then double-click the document's icon to open it in its application.

Moving shortcuts

2. Because all your current work is in this folder, you want it at the top of the Other Shortcuts group. Point to the Projects folder, hold down the left mouse button, and drag the folder upward, releasing the mouse button when the black position bar is above My Computer.

After we have added shortcuts to a group, we may want to change the group's name to reflect its shortcuts. Try this:

Renaming groups

1. Right-click a blank area of the Outlook bar and choose Rename Group from the object menu.

2. With Other Shortcuts highlighted on its button, type *Work* and press Enter.

To avoid confusion, we had better reverse our steps here and return the Outlook bar to its original status. Here are the steps:

1. Repeat steps 1 and 2 above to return the group's name to *Other Shortcuts*.

2. Right-click the Projects icon in the Outlook bar and choose Remove From Outlook Bar from the object menu, clicking Yes to confirm the deletion.

Adding and removing groups

If you want to add a group to the Outlook bar, right-click the bar and choose Add New Group from the object menu. Then type the name of the new group and press Enter. If you want to remove a group, you right-click the appropriate group's button and choose Remove Group from the object menu. Click Yes to confirm that you want to delete the group.

3. Click the My Computer icon, double-click the icon for your hard drive, right-click the Projects folder, and choose Delete from the object menu to erase the demonstration folder. If necessary, click Yes to confirm the deletion.

Well, that wraps up our discussion of the ways you can modify Outlook's views. But before we end this chapter, we'll take a quick look at how to get help if you get stuck.

Getting Help

This tour of Outlook has covered a lot of ground in just a few pages, and you might be wondering how anyone could possibly remember it all. Don't worry. If we forget how to carry out a particular task, help is never far away. We've already seen how the ScreenTips feature can jog our memory about the functions of the toolbar buttons. And you may have noticed that each dialog box has a Help button (the question mark in the top right corner) that provides information about its options. Here, we'll take a look at ways to get information using the Office Assistant, which has probably popped up a few times during this chapter. Follow these steps:

1. Click the Notes icon in the Outlook Shortcuts group and click the Office Assistant button on the toolbar. The Office Assistant appears, giving you several options, as shown here:

The Office Assistant button

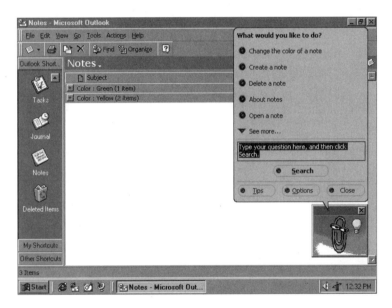

The Office Assistant's options reflect the work you have been doing. If you don't find any of the current options helpful, you can type a question in the Search box and then click the Search button to have the Office Assistant look for topics that most closely match your question.

2. Type *How do I change views?* and click the Search button. The Office Assistant displays a list of related topics.

3. Click the Change The View option to display the Help window shown on the next page. (Outlook may take a few seconds to prepare the Help file.)

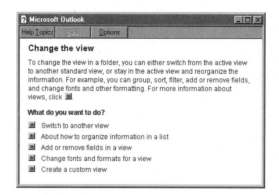

4. Read through the information and then click the arrow button to the left of Change Fonts And Formats For A View to display instructions on how to complete the task.

5. Click the Back button to move back to the Change The View topic, and then explore other options.

6. Click the Help window's Close button and then click the Office Assistant's Close button.

If you prefer to get help without the aid of the Office Assistant, you can use the Help menu. Follow these steps:

1. Choose Contents And Index from the Help menu and, if necessary, click the Index tab to display this dialog box:

2. In the edit box, type *views*. The list below scrolls to display topics beginning with the letters you type.

3. Select Changing in the list of Views index entries, and then click the Display button. Then select Change The View in the Topics Found window and click Display again. Help displays the information shown on the facing page.

4. Click the Close button.

The Contents tab of the Outlook Help dialog box organizes information into broad categories. You might want to try using the Find tab, which searches the text of the topics to find a word or words you enter, instead of relying on topic headings. We'll leave you to explore other Help topics on your own, either now or as you need them.

Quitting Outlook

Well, that's a lot of work for one chapter, and we're ready for a break. All that's left is to show you how to end an Outlook session. Usually, we'll have to quit only once a day, because it is convenient to start Outlook and then minimize it when it's not in use, quitting the program only when we're ready to go home at the end of the day. That way, we can take full advantage of Outlook's capabilities to periodically check e-mail, remind us of appointments, and display notes. When we are ready to quit Outlook for the day, here's what we do:

1. Choose Exit from the File menu.

Here are some other ways to quit Outlook:

- Click the Close button at the right end of Outlook's title bar.

- Press Alt, then F (the underlined letter in *File* on the menu bar), then X (the underlined letter in *Exit* on the File menu).

- Double-click the Control menu icon (the envelope/clock icon) at the left end of Outlook's title bar.

Using the Web for help

If you have a modem and are connected to the Internet, you can quickly access Microsoft's Web site to get help or technical support. Simply choose Microsoft On The Web from the Help menu to display a submenu, and then choose the appropriate option.

2
Managing Contacts

The contacts list is the heart of any information management system. In this chapter, we show you how to add contact information and how to organize the contacts list and view its information in various ways. Then we customize the contact form to include new items of information.

*Create a custom form
that includes special
information fields*

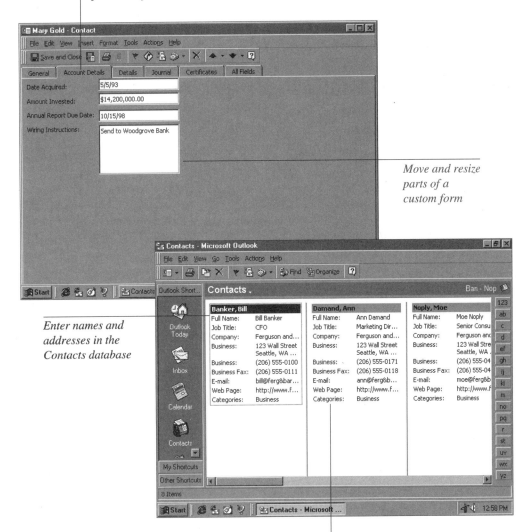

*Move and resize
parts of a
custom form*

*Enter names and
addresses in the
Contacts database*

*Explore different
ways to view the
Contacts database*

uring the work day, we do things that involve other people, such as sending e-mail messages, scheduling meetings, or tracking tasks and projects. We need to store information about the people we frequently interact with in some type of database that holds the many kinds of information important to our daily relationships.

The Contacts component of Outlook performs the tasks of an electronic address book. We can look up addresses when writing letters or sending invoices or reports, and our computer can dial phone numbers for us. But Contacts also stores e-mail addresses and Web site URLs and allocates space for additional information about each contact. What's more, we can designate important contacts for automatic journal tracking so that all interactions with them are logged.

In this chapter, we'll look at the Contacts component and explore many of its features. As you will see, developing a contacts list when we first start using Outlook helps streamline activities performed in other Outlook components. Let's display the contents of Contacts in the workspace now:

The Contacts icon

1. If necessary, start Outlook by double-clicking its desktop icon.

2. Click the Contacts icon in the Outlook Shortcuts group on the Outlook bar to display its contents in the workspace, like this:

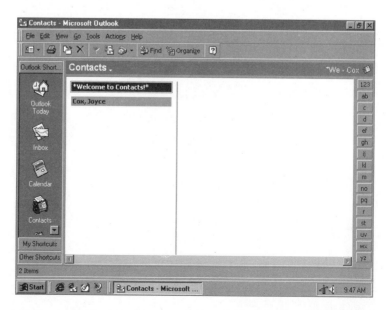

Because we have not used Contacts before, our list consists of two entries, called *address cards*, that have been created by Outlook: one labeled *Welcome to Contacts* and one labeled with the name of the person licensed to use Outlook on this computer. Down the right side of the workspace are buttons, like the tabs in a standard address book, that we click to move from one section of the contacts database to another.

Address cards

Adding Contacts

Creating a contacts list is easy. In this section, we build a list for a fictional money management firm called Ferguson and Bardell. Let's add a few contacts to the list in the workspace:

1. Click the New Contact button on the toolbar to display this address-card window:

The New Contact button

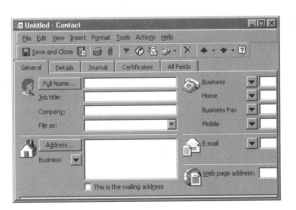

2. If necessary, maximize the window, and then type *Mona Terry* in the first edit box. (You can click the Full Name button to make sure Outlook has accurately broken down the name into its component parts—first and last names, for example—for use when creating documents such as form letters.) Notice that Outlook has entered *Terry, Mona* in the File As box for sorting purposes. (You can change this entry to *Mona Terry* by clicking the arrow to the right of the box.)

3. Type *Senior Consultant* in the Job Title edit box and then type *Ferguson and Bardell* in the Company edit box.

4. Click the arrow to the left of any of the edit boxes in the Phone section and notice that you can reassign the boxes to record

Importing and exporting contacts

If you have created a list of names and addresses in Access, Schedule+, or Word, you can import it into Contacts. Choose Import And Export from the File menu, select the desired action from the Import And Export Wizard, and click Next. Select a format from the file type list and click Next. Click the Browse button, navigate to the desired file, and click OK. Then select a duplicates option and click Next. Select Contacts as the destination folder and click Next again. Click the Map Custom Fields button, match fields from the source file with those that are in the destination file, and click OK. Then in the last dialog box, click Finish to import the database. To export a list from Contacts to another program, follow the same procedure, selecting the desired export option in the first dialog box.

the ways you can get in touch with this contact. Press Esc to close the list of possibilities without reassigning any boxes.

5. Enter *2065550222* as the Business number and *2065550223* as the Business Fax number. Notice that Outlook inserts the appropriate parentheses and hyphens.

6. In the Address box, type *123 Wall Street,* press Enter, and type *Seattle, WA 98105.* (Click the Address button to check that the address is correctly broken down into its component parts.) If you wanted, you could click the arrow to the right of Business, assign a different type to the edit box, and enter another address for this contact. Because you have entered only one address, Outlook assumes this is the mailing address and checks this option.

Entering multiple addresses

7. Enter *mona@ferg&bard.biz* in the E-mail edit box. (You can enter up to three e-mail addresses by clicking the arrow and assigning a new type, and you can search for e-mail addresses in an existing address book by clicking the Address Book button to the right of the edit box.)

8. Finally, enter *www.ferg&bard.biz* in the Web Page Address edit box. Outlook converts the address to an active Internet link, and your screen should now look like this:

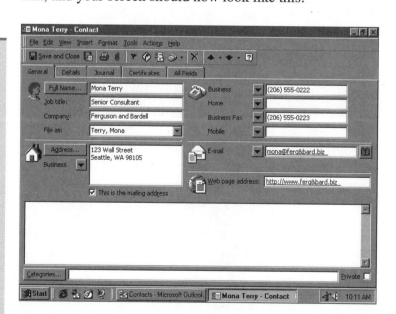

Other ways to add new contacts

If you are working in another Outlook component and want to quickly add a new contact, you can choose New and then Contact from the File menu. If you have installed the Office shortcut bar (see the tip on page 8), you can click its New Contact button. If you prefer to use keyboard shortcuts, press Ctrl+N to enter a new contact from within the Contacts component or press Ctrl+Shift+C to enter a new contact from another Outlook component.

9. To assign Mona Terry to the business category, click the Categories button in the bottom left corner of the window to display the Categories dialog box shown earlier on page 12. Then click the Business check box and click OK.

The Save And New button

10. Click the Save And New button to save the current address card and display a blank address-card window.

11. Create address cards for the people listed below, typing *Ferguson and Bardell* as the company name, *123 Wall Street, Seattle, WA 98105* as the address, and *www.ferg&bard.biz* as the Web address for all of the contacts. Assign them all to the business category. Click the Save And Close button after the last one.

Name	Sue Ply	Ann Damand	Bill Banker	Moe Noply
Job Title	Financial Analyst	Marketing Director	CFO	Senior Consultant
Bus. Phone	2065550112	2065550117	2065550100	2065550441
Bus. Fax	2065550114	2065550118	2065550111	2065550444
E-mail	sue@ferg&bard.biz	ann@ferg&bard.biz	bill@ferg&bard.biz	moe@ferg&bard.biz

Editing and Adding Information

Once we add an address card to our contacts list, we can easily edit the information on the card by double-clicking the card in the workspace to redisplay the address-card window. Looking over the address cards now in the workspace, suppose we discover an error in the Ann Damand card. Here's how to edit existing contact information:

1. Double-click *Damand, Ann* to display her address card.

Displaying an address-card window

2. Change *0117* in the phone number to *0171* and click Save And Close.

   You may have noticed that the address-card window is multi-tabbed. We used the General tab to fill in the information shown earlier. If we want to add more information about a contact, such as an assistant's name or a birthday, we can use the Details tab. (For information about the Journal tab, see the tip on page 39, and for information about the All Fields

Editing in the workspace

If you need to make one or two minor changes to the information visible in the workspace, simply click an insertion point and make the changes, without displaying the address card window. (In some views, you may not be able to edit certain fields; try another view.)

and Certificates tabs, see the tip on pages 40 and 41.) Let's add some personal information for Mona Terry, who is not only a colleague but a friend. Follow these steps:

Recording special occasions

1. Double-click *Terry, Mona* in the workspace and then click the Details tab to display these address-card options:

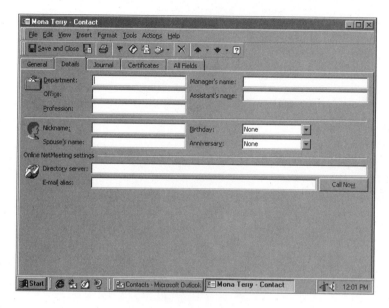

2. Click the arrow to the right of the Birthday box to display a small calendar.

3. Use the arrows on either side of the current month's name to navigate to December. Then click 28.

4. Repeat this procedure for the Anniversary box, setting it to August 7.

5. Click an insertion point in the Spouse's Name edit box and type *Sandy*. Then click Save And Close.

Deleting Contacts

To keep a contacts list up-to-date, once in a while we need to delete address cards. Try this:

1. If your contacts list includes a Welcome to Contacts card, click its header to select it, and then click the Delete button.

More about entering birthdays

When you enter a contact's birthday or anniversary, the date is recorded in the Calendar component of Outlook. (We discuss Calendar in detail in Chapter 4.) Because of this feature, you'll no longer have to record special occasions in several places, and you'll never forget these important dates again!

2. Delete any other contacts shown in the list when you first displayed it, leaving only the five you just entered. The contacts list now looks like the one shown here:

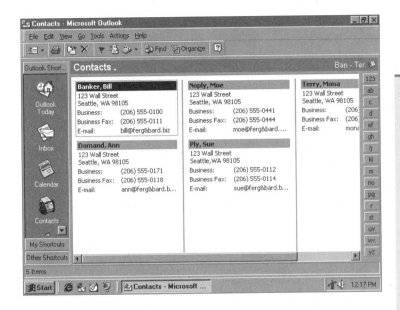

Organizing Contacts

As your contacts list grows, you will probably want to organize it so that it is easier to use. In Chapter 1, we looked at different ways to view notes, and many of the techniques we used with Notes can be applied to Contacts. In this section, we will look at other organizational options that are relevant to the Contacts component.

Before we experiment with organizing contacts, let's add some more address cards. Then we'll have more contacts to organize. Follow these steps:

1. Click the New Contact button to display the address-card window shown earlier.

2. Enter the names and addresses on the following page, clicking the Save And New button to start a new address card and clicking the Save And Close button after the last entry.

The Journal tab

You use the Journal tab of the address-card window to track interactions with a particular contact. (We discuss the Journal component in detail in Chapter 6.) With Outlook, you can manually record activities such as sending e-mail messages, creating letters in Word, making phone calls (if Outlook dials them for you), and requesting meetings, or you can have the program record them automatically. To manually record an item for a contact, open the contact's address card, click the Journal tab, and then click the New Journal Entry button. To automatically record items, display the Journal tab for the desired contact, then click the Automatically Record Journal Entries For This Contact check box, and click Save And Close. (Select this option only for your most important contacts; otherwise, your Outlook database can grow quite large.) To specify what items and file types are to be recorded for a particular contact, first choose Options from the Tools menu and then click the Preferences tab. Next, click the Journal Options button, select a contact in the For These Contacts list, and select and deselect various recording options.

Name	Ima Tripp	Al Pine	Rocky Rhode
Job Title	President	President	President
Company	Exotic Excursions	Fabrikam, Inc.	Sweet Forgiveness
Address	505 West Ave.	1200 Yukon Ave.	1540 Iceberg Drive
	Seattle, WA 98115	Anchorage, AK 99502	Seattle, WA 98122
Bus. Phone	2065554856	9075551454	2065551500
Bus. Fax	2065554782	9075551451	2065551501
E-mail	ima@ex-ex.biz	al@fabrikam.biz	rocky@sweet.biz
Web Address	www.ex-ex.biz	www.fabrikam.biz	www.sweet.biz

Creating New Categories

We've completed all the address cards, and now we need to fine-tune their categories. Some of the contacts we just added are clients but they are also members of a professional organization we belong to. Let's create a new category for them:

1. Scroll the workspace, double-click *Tripp, Ima*, and then in the address-card window, click the Categories button.

2. Click the Master Category List button in the bottom right corner to display this dialog box:

The All Fields tab

When you click the All Fields tab of an address-card window, Outlook displays the available fields in a table. To display alternative fields, click the arrow to the right of the Select From box and select a different category. You can enter information about the contact by typing text in the Value column. You can also create new fields from this tab by clicking the New button at the bottom of the tab.

3. In the New Category edit box, type *BusNet* and click Add. Outlook adds the new category to the list.

4. Click OK to return to the Categories dialog box. Click the BusNet check box to select it and click OK.

5. To save your changes, click Save And Close.

6. Now double-click *Pine, Al*, click the Categories button, select BusNet, click OK, and then click Save And Close.

7. Repeat step 6 for Rocky Rhode's card.

Switching Views

By default, Outlook displays the contacts list in Address Cards view, where some of the pertinent information about our contacts appears on index cards that are sorted alphabetically. Because this list is small, we can easily scroll through the cards. However, as a contacts list grows, viewing the list in a different way may be more efficient. Let's explore the other available views now:

1. Choose Current View and then Detailed Address Cards from the View menu. The contacts information now looks like this:

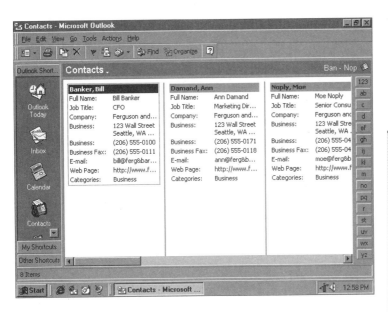

In this view, Outlook displays all the information that was entered on the General tab of the address-card window.

2. Choose Phone List from the Current View submenu to display your contacts as shown at the top of the next page.

The Certificates tab

Certificates (also called *digital IDs*) are used primariliy by companies that want to maintain secure computing environments. You obtain a certificate from an independent organization such as Verisign, Inc., and then you attach it to your e-mail messages to prove your identity. If you want to exchange encrypted messages with contacts, you need copies of their certificates. You can ask them to send you messages with their certificates attached, and can then reply to those messages to store the certificates in the respective contact address cards (see online help for more information).

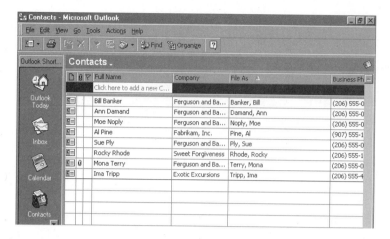

This table view displays identifying information for each contact as well as four phone columns, which might not contain numbers. (To add a new contact in this view, click the top row and type the information.) In a table view, you can see that the contacts list is really a database, where the information about a particular contact is stored in a *record* (row) and an individual item of information is stored in a *field* (column).

3. The remaining four table views display contacts sorted by category, company, location, and follow-up tag. Try each view in turn, finishing up with the By Category view.

4. If necessary, click the plus sign next to each category to display your contacts like this:

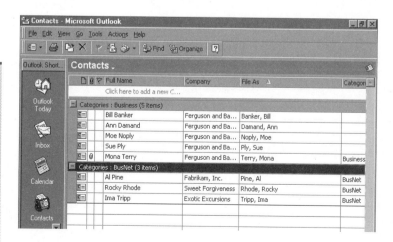

Sorting in table view

You can sort the information in a table view by clicking the header at the top of the column by which you want Outlook to sort. An arrow appears in the header, pointing up if the column is sorted in ascending order or down if it is sorted in descending order. Clicking the header again reverses the order.

Creating a Custom View

The By Category view organizes our contacts conveniently but has a couple of drawbacks: it doesn't display addresses, and it repeats some information. We showed you one method for customizing a view on page 19, but let's try another method:

1. Because we are in By Category view, the Categories field is redundant. So let's get rid of it by right-clicking the Categories column header and choosing Remove This Column from the object menu.

Deleting columns

2. Repeat step 1 to remove the empty Home Phone and Mobile Phone columns. (You will need to scroll them into view to delete them.)

3. To resize the Full Name column so that it is just wide enough to fit the longest name, right-click the column header and choose Best Fit from the object menu.

Resizing columns

4. To resize the File As column, position the mouse pointer over the column header's right border, and when the pointer changes to a double-headed arrow, double-click the left mouse button. The column instantly adjusts its width to fit the longest entry. The Contacts window now looks something like this:

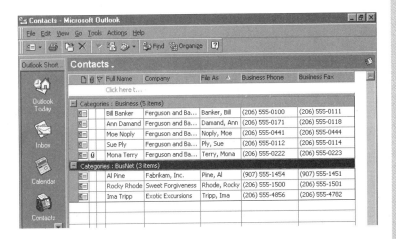

Flagging contacts for follow-up

If you need to do something concerning a contact, you can click the contact's flag column in a table view and select Flagged from the drop-down list to display a small flag to the left of the contact's name. You can also select the contact and either click the Flag For Follow Up button on the toolbar or choose Flag For Follow Up from the Actions menu to display a dialog box in which you can specify why you are flagging the contact and whether you want to be reminded about this task.

The custom view is starting to take shape, but now we need to add some columns. Follow these steps:

Adding columns

1. To add a column, right-click a column header and choose Field Chooser from the object menu to display this dialog box:

2. Click the Business Address box to select it, point to it, hold down the left mouse button, and drag to the column header row. In the row, a red arrow indicates the new field's location. Release the mouse button when the box sits between the Company and File As column headers.

3. Repeat step 2 to add an E-mail column at the right end of the table. (Scroll the end of the table into view first.) Then click the Field Chooser's Close button.

4. Resize the Business Address and E-mail columns so that they display all of their information.

With those adjustments complete, we're ready to save the current settings as a new view. Follow these steps:

Saving a new view

1. Choose Current View and then Define Views from the View menu to display the dialog box shown earlier on page 21.

2. With Current View Settings selected, click the Copy button to display the Copy View dialog box.

3. Type *New By Category* in the Name Of New View edit box, check All Contact Folders in the Can Be Used On section, and click OK.

4. Click OK in the View Summary dialog box, and click Apply View in the Define Views dialog box.

5. To restore the original By Category view, choose Current View and then Define Views from the View menu, click By Category in the View list, click the Reset button, and click OK. Then click Close to close the dialog box.

Restoring a view's settings

6. To confirm that the new view is now available, choose Current View from the View menu and check that New By Category is the selection on its submenu. Press Esc three times to close the menus.

Creating Your Own Contact Form

On page 38, we added a contact's birthday, anniversary, and spouse's name on the Details tab of the address-card window. As we work with the Contacts component of Outlook, we may find that the General and Details tabs provide some fields that we don't need and don't provide some that we do need. To ensure that the contacts list includes precisely the fields we need, we can develop a custom contact form.

In this section, we'll develop a custom form for the clients of Ferguson and Bardell. Creating forms in Outlook is similar to creating them in Microsoft Access. If you are familiar with that process, you will recognize the techniques we discuss here. If you are not familiar with the Access process, this section will give you enough experience to experiment later, when you've identified the forms you will need for your work. Let's start by displaying the window where we'll design our form:

1. Click the New Contact button on the toolbar to display a blank address-card window, and then choose Forms and Design This Form from the Tools menu. Outlook displays the address-card window in design view and opens the Field Chooser box, as shown on the next page. (If Outlook does not display the Field Chooser box, choose the command from the Form menu.)

Switching to design view

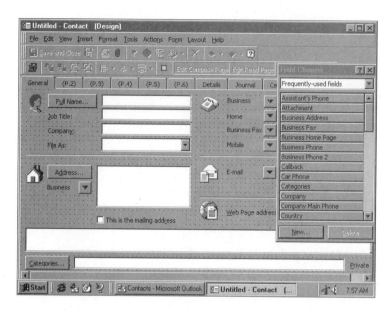

As you can see, the design-view window has more tabs than the information-entry window.

2. Click the (P.2) tab to display a blank second page.

We can now design the form by dragging fields from the Field Chooser box to the page displayed in the window. If none of the predefined fields fit the bill, we can create new fields. Let's add some new fields now:

Creating new fields ▶ 1. Click the New button in the Field Chooser box to display this New Field dialog box:

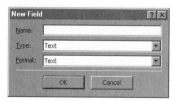

Editing custom forms

To edit an existing custom form, first open it by choosing it from the Actions menu. Switch to design view by choosing Forms and then Design This Form from the Tools menu. Make any editing adjustments and click the Publish Form button on the Design toolbar to save the form with the changes.

2. Type *Date Acquired* in the Name edit box.

3. Click the arrow to the right of the Type box and select Date/Time.

4. Select the short date format (6/1/98, for example) from the Format drop-down list and click OK. In the Field Chooser box, Outlook displays the User-Defined Fields In Folder group and adds a Date Acquired field box to the group list.

5. Repeat steps 1 through 4 to add the fields shown here:

Name	*Amount Invested*	*Annual Report Due Date*	*Wiring Instructions*
Type	*Currency*	*Date/Time*	*Text*
Format	*Dollars and Cents*	*Short Date*	*Text*

To add the new fields to the blank form, follow these steps:

1. Click the Date Acquired field in the Field Chooser box and drag it anywhere on the blank form. When you release the mouse button, Outlook positions the new field in the top left corner of the form. ◄——— Adding fields to a new form

2. Next, drag the Amount Invested field onto the form. Outlook positions the field below the Date Acquired field.

3. Drag the Annual Report Due Date and Wiring Instructions fields onto the form and then close the Field Chooser box. The form now looks like this:

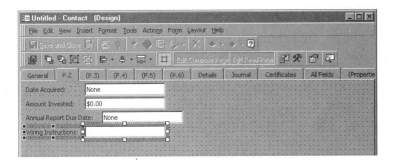

The form is made up of two types of boxes. The boxes containing the field names are called *labels*, and the white boxes—where we will enter information in the new form—are called *controls*. ◄——— Labels and controls

Moving Controls and Labels

Moving the fields onto the new form was easy enough, but Outlook has simply dumped everything in the top left corner. Let's line up the controls to make them easier to work with:

1. Click the white control to the right of Date Acquired. Small squares called *handles* appear around the control's border, indicating that it is selected.

2. Hold down the Ctrl key and click the three remaining control boxes so that all of them are selected, like this:

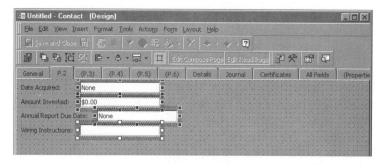

The Align button

More layout options

When creating a custom contact form, you may want to explore some of the other available commands on the Layout menu. For example, you can adjust the space between objects by selecting the objects and then using the Horizontal Spacing or Vertical Spacing commands. You can also quickly size objects to the width of their text by selecting the object and choosing Size To Fit from the Layout menu. If you don't like the effect of a particular command, choose Undo from the Edit menu.

3. Choose Align and then Left from the Layout menu. (You can also click the arrow to the right of the Align button on the Design toolbar and select Left.) Outlook simultaneously aligns all of the selected controls to the left, as shown here:

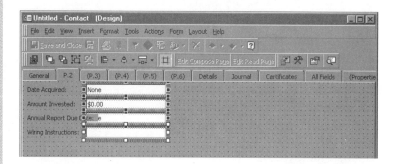

Does the Annual Report Due Date label partially obscure its control? To fix this problem, we'll fine-tune the position of the controls with the mouse. Follow the steps at the top of the facing page.

1. Click a blank area of the form to remove the handles.

2. Select the Annual Report Due Date control, point to its border (not a handle), and when the pointer changes to a four-headed arrow, hold down the left mouse button and drag the control to the right by at least three gridline markers.

Moving controls

3. Repeat the previous step to move the three remaining controls to the right, keeping them all aligned, as shown here:

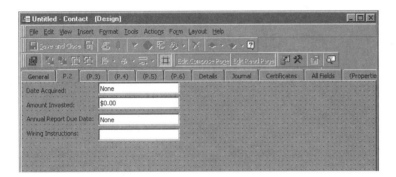

Sizing Controls and Labels

The sizes of the first three controls on the new form are fine, but we need to make the last control larger in order to display lengthy instructions for wiring money. We should also resize the first, second, and fourth labels so that they are the same width as the Annual Report Due Date label. Let's resize these items now:

1. Select the Wiring Instructions control, point to the bottom middle handle, and when the pointer changes to a double-headed arrow, hold down the left mouse button and drag downward until the box approximately triples in size.

2. To make all the labels the same size as the Annual Report Due Date label, select the other three labels by clicking each in turn while holding down the Ctrl key. While still holding the Ctrl key, select the Annual Report Due Date label. (You must select this label last.)

The toolbox

When creating custom forms, you might want to use the toolbox, which is displayed when you click the Control Toolbox button on the Design toolbar. You can use the toolbox buttons to add different types of controls to a form. For example, you can add text boxes, labels, option buttons, check boxes, graphics, and frames. You might want to explore these tools and practice adding form objects. Check online help for details about these tools so that you can use them to create forms that meet your needs.

3. Choose Make Same Size and then Width from the Layout menu to tell Outlook to resize all the labels to match the last label you selected. Click somewhere else to deselect the labels, and the form now looks like this:

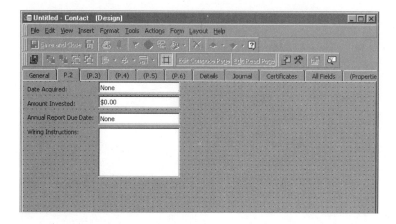

Saving a New Form

This simple form is now complete, and all we have to do is save it so that we can begin to use it. But first we'll give the form's tab a more descriptive name than P.2. Follow these steps:

Renaming a page ➤ 1. Choose Rename Page from the Form menu to display this dialog box:

2. Type *Account Details* as the name and then click OK. Outlook displays the new name on the tab.

The Publish Form button ➤ 3. To save the new form, click the Publish Form button at the left end of the Design toolbar. Outlook does not allow you to change its default contact form, so it displays the dialog box shown at the top of the facing page so that you can save the form with a different name.

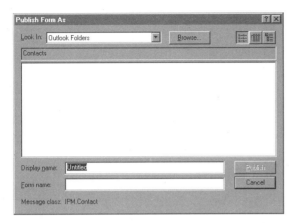

4. Type *Client Form* as the form name and, with Outlook Folders in the Look In box and Contacts in the header above the empty list box, click Publish.

Filling In Custom Forms

Now that we have created and saved the custom form, we can use it to enter a new contact. Follow these steps:

1. Choose Run This Form from the Form menu. Outlook opens an address-card window that reflects the work you just did in design view.

2. On the General tab, enter the following contact information:

Name	*Mary Gold*
Job Title	*President*
Company	*Terra Firm*
Address	*1440 West Dogwood Road*
	Cedar Rapids, IA 52401
Bus. Phone	*3195558563*
Bus. Fax	*3195558560*
E-mail	*mary@t-firm.biz*
Web Address	*www.t-firm.biz*
Category	*BusNet*

3. Click the Account Details tab and in the Date Acquired box, replace the word *None* with *5/5/93*.

Hiding form pages

If you want to keep a custom form simple by not displaying some tabs in the address-card window, click a tab to display it in design view and then choose Display This Page from the Form menu to toggle the command off. Any tabs that have names in parentheses —(P.3), for example—are not displayed in the address-card window unless you have customized them, so you can hide only the General, Details, Journal, Certificates, and All Fields tabs.

4. Press Tab and type *14,200,000.00*. Press Tab again, type *10/15/98*, press Tab, and type *Send to Woodgrove Bank*. The Account Details tab now looks like this:

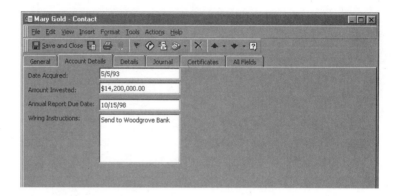

5. Click Save And Close to close the new contact.

6. Click the window's Close button to exit design view, clicking No to discard the blank address card you opened on page 45.

Opening a custom form to enter a new contact →

To use the custom client form to enter new contacts, choose the New Client Form command from the Actions menu instead of clicking the New Contact button. To set your custom form as the default, right-click the Contacts icon in the Outlook bar, choose Properties, and on the General tab, select the desired form from the When Posting drop-down list and click OK.

Using Contacts to Write a Letter

As we work our way through the rest of this book, we will periodically introduce ways to use the contacts list to speed up other Outlook tasks, such as sending an e-mail message, planning a meeting, or adding a new task. And having developed a contacts list, we can open Microsoft Word and use the Address Book when writing letters or creating mailing labels. (See the tip on the facing page.)

Even if Word is installed on our computer, sometimes it is easier to write a letter directly from Outlook's Contacts component. The Letter Wizard accomplishes this feat, walking us through the steps of creating the letter and letting us determine the information we want to include. When we have completed the

Deleting custom forms

To delete custom forms, choose Options from the Tools menu, and on the Other tab, click the Advanced Options button in the General section. Then click Custom Forms, and click the Manage Forms button. (Or you can right-click the Contacts icon in the Outlook bar, choose Properties, and then click the Manage button.) In the Forms Manager dialog box, click an active Set button, navigate to the Contacts folder in the Set Library To dialog box, select it, and click OK. Then select the form you want to remove and click the Delete button. Click Yes to confirm the deletion. Close the dialog boxes.

wizard's dialog boxes, it opens the letter in Microsoft Word so that we can write the text of the letter. Follow these steps to compose a letter to Al Pine.

1. With Contacts open in the workspace, switch to Address Cards view and click the Al Pine address card once to select it.

2. Choose New Letter To Contact from the Actions menu to display this first Letter Wizard dialog box:

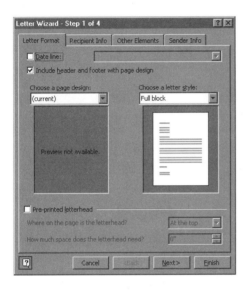

3. Click the Date Line check box so that the letter displays the current date, as shown in the box to the right.

4. In the Choose A Letter Style box, check that Full Block is selected. (The Letter Wizard displays a preview of the style in the box below.)

5. Click the arrow to the right of the Choose A Page Design box and check out the page design options. (Included are Word templates, such as Contemporary Letter and Elegant Letter.) If necessary, select (Current) from the list.

6. Click the Pre-Printed Letterhead check box at the bottom of the dialog box and use the arrows to tell the wizard to allow 1" at the top of the page for a preprinted letterhead. Then click Next to display the Recipient Info tab of the Letter Wizard, as shown at the top of the next page.

The Outlook Address Book

Provided the Outlook Address Book is included in the list of services in the active profile, your contacts list is one of the "address books" available when you create mailing labels in Word. (Choose Services from the Tools menu to check your services list, and click the Add button if you need to add Outlook Address Book to your profile.) The Outlook Address Book stores the information entered in the address-card window. Other available address books might include the Global Address List (created and maintained by your company) and a Personal Address Book, where you keep the information you use most frequently. To create labels or form letters using your contacts list, use Word's mail-merge feature. When you click the Get Data button in the Mail Merge Helper dialog box, choose the Use Address Book option and select the Outlook Address Book. Then continue following the normal mail-merge procedure. (If you need help with the mail-merge feature, consult online help.) If you want to easily insert one of your contact's addresses in a Word document, you can do so by adding an Insert Address button to a Word toolbar. (For information on adding buttons to toolbars, see online help.)

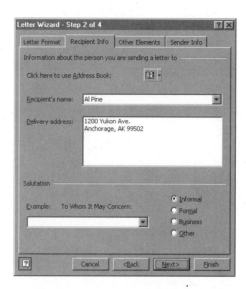

Calling a contact

If a modem is hooked up to your computer, you can have Outlook dial phone numbers of your contacts for you. With Contacts displayed in the workspace, select the contact you want to call and choose Call Contact from the Actions menu to display a submenu of commands. Included on the list are the phone numbers for this contact, a New Call command that you can use to dial a different number, and Redial and Speed Dial commands. Choosing a phone number displays the New Call dialog box. You can have Journal track the phone call by clicking the Create New Journal Entry check box. (See the tip on page 123 for more information.) To dial the number, click the Start Call button, and when the Call Status dialog box appears, pick up the receiver and then click the Talk button. When you finish the phone call, hang up the receiver, click the End Call button, and then click Close in the New Call dialog box.

7. Read over the recipient information, check that the Informal option is selected in the Salutation section, and then click Next to display the Other Elements tab:

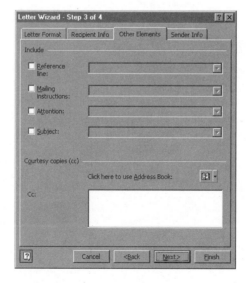

8. Click the Reference Line check box, click the arrow to the right of its box, and select RE:.

9. Click an insertion point to the right of RE: in the edit box, press the Spacebar, and then type *Monthly Lecture Series*. Click Next to display the fourth tab, shown on the facing page.

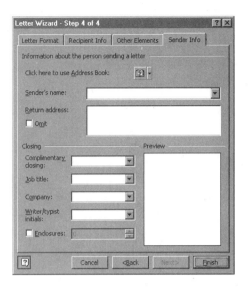

10. Type your name in the Sender's Name box. Then click the arrow to the right of the Complimentary Closing box and select Sincerely from the drop-down list. Click Finish to display the letter in Word, as shown below. (If necessary, close the Office Assistant and maximize the window.)

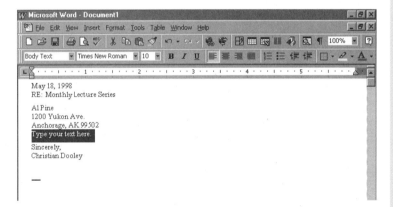

11. We won't actually type the text of the letter now, so click Word's Close button to close the program and the letter, and click No when asked about saving changes.

The Letter Wizard gives you some idea of the ways you can streamline your work by using the contacts list. If you want to use Outlook to its full potential, be sure to keep your contacts list up-to-date!

Printing the contacts list

Using Outlook eliminates some of the need for paper printouts, but when you want a printout of your contacts list, click the Print button to display the Print dialog box. Here, you can select from several layout choices in the Print Style section, and you can click the Page Setup button to make adjustments on the Format, Paper, or Header/Footer tabs. On the Paper tab of the Page Setup dialog box, you can change the Type setting in the Paper section to Avery Labels or FiloFax, and you can change the Size setting in the Page section to fit special formats for Franklin Planners, Day Timers, or Day Runners. As you make modifications, you can check what the printout will look like by clicking the Print Preview button. In print preview, the mouse pointer changes to a magnifying glass. Click the mouse button once to zoom in on the page and click again to zoom back out. In the Print dialog box, you can also click the Define Styles button to make permanent edits to a particular style or to copy a style. When you are ready to print, simply click OK in the Print dialog box.

3

Communicating
with E-Mail

Whether you're working on a stand-alone computer or on a network, this chapter shows you how to use Outlook's e-mail component to send, read and respond to e-mail messages. Then we look at ways to organize messages for maximum efficiency.

*Compose messages offline
and send them to the
Outbox for later delivery*

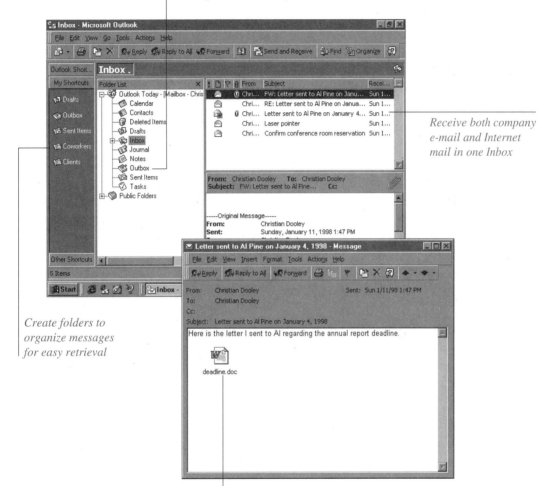

*Receive both company
e-mail and Internet
mail in one Inbox*

*Create folders to
organize messages
for easy retrieval*

*Attach files to e-mail
messages for transmitting
to one or more recipients*

Setting up Internet e-mail

If you work for a large organization or you access the Internet through a school computer, e-mail has probably already been set up on your computer. If you are working on a stand-alone computer, you can't send or receive Internet e-mail in Outlook until you set it up. You will need to obtain the domain names of your outgoing e-mail server and incoming e-mail server from your ISP. Then start the Internet Connection Wizard by choosing Settings and then Control Panel from the Start menu, double-clicking the Internet icon and clicking the Connection tab of the Internet Properties dialog box. In the Connection section, click the Connect button to start the wizard. As you work through the dialog boxes, you will need to enter information such as your e-mail address, POP account name, password, and your connection type. If you need help with this setup, contact your ISP for specific instructions. If you already have a Dial-Up Networking connection to your ISP, you may need to add the Internet E-Mail service to your Outlook profile. Choose Services from the Tools menu and complete all the tabs of the dialog box to set up this service.

O utlook's Contacts component, discussed in Chapter 2, helps us organize information about people without actually communicating with them. But communication with colleagues is an integral part of our daily work, and in recent years, electronic mail (or *e-mail*) has become the primary method of communication for many of us. Some people have internal e-mail (company-wide or institution-wide), some have Internet e-mail, and some have both. Regardless of what type of e-mail we have, it can all be handled by Outlook's e-mail component, and in this chapter, we discuss how to use this component to create, send, receive, and manage e-mail messages.

There's nothing difficult about the concept of e-mail. It's simply a way of sending messages that bypasses the traditional post office. The beauty of e-mail is that it doesn't use paper resources, it's fast, and it costs nothing (at least, nothing more than we may already be paying for Internet access). Sometimes it is even better than using the telephone because we can deal with important business right away rather than running the risk of playing phone tag. Add to these advantages the fact that we can include files, programs, and other attachments with the messages we send, and the fact that we can send the same message to several people without any additional effort, and it's easy to understand why people with abysmal letter-writing habits become staunch advocates of e-mail as a means of communication.

Sometimes people confuse internal e-mail and Internet e-mail, and it's easy to understand why because in many ways, they are similar. However, having internal e-mail doesn't necessarily mean we have Internet e-mail, and vice versa. To be able to send e-mail to a colleague down the hall via internal e-mail, both our computer and our colleague's computer need to be connected to the company's or the institution's network. To be able to send e-mail to a client in another state via the Internet, both our computer and our client's computer need to be able to access the Internet. This access may be invisibly provided by a server on our network, further blurring the distinction between internal and Internet e-mail. Or access may be more visibly provided via a modem connection to an *Internet service provider* (or *ISP*). Either way, we can use Outlook's e-mail component. Outlook can be configured to work with many of the more popular e-mail programs, but to take full advantage of some of Outlook's capabilities, we need to be working on a network that runs Microsoft Exchange Server. (See the tip on the facing page for information about setting up Outlook to access an Internet e-mail account.)

Using Inbox

As you may recall from Chapter 1, by default Inbox is the component displayed in the workspace when we start Outlook. Inbox is Outlook's main e-mail folder and the place where we will spend most of our time when working with e-mail. Let's take a closer look at Inbox now:

1. If necessary, start Outlook by double-clicking its icon on the desktop. One of two things happens:

- If you are working on a network and Outlook is set up to automatically log on to an internal e-mail server when it starts, Outlook connects to the server and checks for new messages. (For more information about automatic logon, see the tip on this page.)

- If you are working on a network and Outlook is not set up to automatically log on to an e-mail server, or if you have only Internet e-mail, Outlook does not connect to your server. (By the way, this method is called *working offline*.) Don't worry though. We can still proceed, and we will show you how to manually make the connection by clicking the Send and Receive button on page 66.

2. Click My Shortcuts at the bottom of the Outlook bar to display its group of icons, which include Drafts, Outbox, and Sent Items. (You can use the Drafts folder to store unsent items.) For now we'll focus on Inbox, leaving our discussion of the other e-mail folders until later in the chapter.

Setting up automatic logon

If you are working on a company network and you need to set up Outlook so that it automatically connects to your e-mail server when you turn on your computer, first choose Options from the Tools menu. On the Mail Services tab, select an option in the Check For New Mail On box, and click OK.

The Inbox icon

3. Click the Outlook Shortcuts button, and if necessary, click the Inbox icon on the Outlook bar to display its contents in the workspace, which looks something like the one on page 7.

In the top pane of the workspace on the right side of the window is a list of the e-mail messages you have received. In the bottom pane, Outlook displays the contents of the selected message. (If this is the first time you've used Inbox and Outlook is not set up to automatically log on to your e-mail server, your workspace may be empty.)

Composing Messages

With Outlook, we both send and receive e-mail through Inbox. We'll look at the sending side of the equation first. For demonstration purposes, we will e-mail a reminder message to ourselves, but bear in mind that we would probably use the Notes or Tasks component for this type of reminder, rather than e-mail. In our examples, we will use company e-mail, but if you are using Internet e-mail, you should have no difficulty following along.

For this example, suppose we are planning a meeting with a client and we want to remind ourselves to check on the conference room reservation first thing tomorrow morning. Follow these steps:

The New Mail Message button

1. Click the New Mail Message button on the toolbar to display a window like the one shown here:

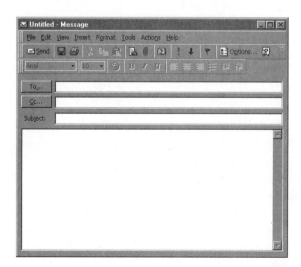

2. In the To edit box, type your own e-mail address. (To send a message to someone else, enter his or her address. To send the same message to more than one person, enter their addresses one after the other, separated by semicolons.) Press Tab.

Sending a message to more than one person

3. To send a courtesy copy of the message, you can enter the name of the recipient in the Cc edit box. For this message, leave the Cc edit box blank by pressing Tab.

Sending courtesy copies

4. In the Subject edit box, type *Confirm conference room reservation*, and press Tab.

Specifying the subject

5. Enter the message itself in the blank area at the bottom of the window. Type *Check on conference room B reservation. It should be reserved at 1:00 PM for two hours. Make sure overhead projector is set up.* Your screen now looks like this:

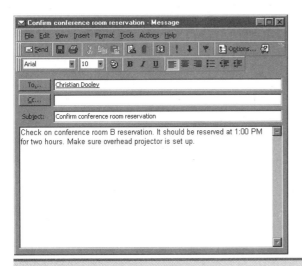

Message options

When composing a new message, you can set message options by clicking the Options button on the toolbar. In the Message Settings section, specify the importance and sensitivity levels of the message. Specifying the importance level as high displays an exclamation mark in the message's header. (You can also set the importance level by clicking the Importance: High or Importance: Low buttons on the toolbar). You can set the sensitivity level to Normal, Personal, Private, or Confidential. In the Security section, select Encrypt Contents And Attachments to make a message's contents readable only by its recipients (as long as the recipient has a compatible encryption program), and select Add Digital Signature to ensure that the message is not altered by someone else. In the Voting And Tracking Options section, set voting options (see the tip on the next page) and specify notification options. In the Delivery Options section, specify locations for replies and for the sent message, and set a delivery date/time and an expiration date for the message. (The message is deleted if not opened by this date.) Also on this tab, you can assign a message to a category by clicking the Categories button and making a selection.

The Send button

6. Send the message by clicking the Send button. Outlook closes the Message window and does one of two things:

   • If you are connected to your e-mail server, Outlook transfers the message to Outbox and, from there, quickly sends it on its way.

   • If you are not connected to your e-mail server, Outlook stores the message in Outbox until your next connection.

The Outbox icon

7. If you are in the latter group, confirm that the message is waiting to be sent by clicking My Shortcuts and then Outbox on the Outlook bar to display the window shown here:

8. Redisplay Inbox's contents by displaying the Outlook Shortcuts group and then clicking the Inbox icon on the Outlook bar.

Adding a signature

To add information to the end of all of your messages, choose Options from the Tools menu and on the Mail Format tab, click the Signature Picker button and click New. Enter a name for the signature and click Next. Type your information in the text box, format it, and click Finish. Click OK in the Signature Picker dialog box. Verify the default signature and click OK. To change the default for a message, click the Signature button and make your selection.

Voting

You can send e-mail messages that include voting buttons so that coworkers can vote on issues. To insert voting buttons in a message, display a new message window and click the Options button on the toolbar. Click the Use Voting Buttons check box in the Voting And Tracking Options section and then click the arrow to the right of its edit box to select the voting button names you want. To use your own button names, type the names you want in the edit box, separating each name with a semicolon. Click Close to close the dialog box and then send the message. When the recipient opens the message, Outlook displays the voting buttons at the top of the message window. They can then click the desired button and either send the response immediately or edit the response before sending it.

Addressing Messages Quickly

Most people spend most of their e-mailing time sending messages to the same group of people. We discussed the Contacts component in Chapter 2 so that when we got to this chapter, we would already have a contacts list to serve as a database of information about people we deal with repeatedly. As you'll see, when we have a contacts list available, tasks such as sending e-mail messages become much easier. Let's send another message, this time using the contacts list to speed up the process. Follow these steps:

1. First, add an address card for yourself to the contacts list, entering your e-mail address in the E-mail field. (If you need a refresher on creating address cards, see page 35.)

2. Next, display Inbox and click the New Mail Message button to display a window like the one shown on page 60.

3. Click the To... button in the window to display the Select Names dialog box. When you are working on a company network, by default Outlook displays the contents of the Global Address List, a list of all the company e-mail addresses maintained by your e-mail server.

4. To see a list of your contacts, click the arrow to the right of the Show Names From The box and select Contacts under Outlook Address Book. The dialog box changes to look like this:

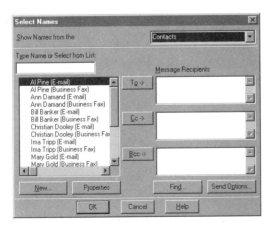

The Personal Address Book

If you find that your Global Address List is cumbersome, or if you frequently send both Internet and internal e-mail, you can use one of several methods to copy often-used addresses to the Personal Address Book. From Inbox, choose Address Book from the Tools menu or click the Address Book button. Select the group you want from the Show Names From The drop-down list, select the person's name in the lower pane and choose Add To Personal Address Book from the File menu. To add an address while in a new message window, click the Address Book button, and in the Select Names dialog box, pick the group and name of the desired addressee, and click the Properties button. Then on the General tab of the E-Mail Properties dialog box, click Personal Address Book in the Add To section. Or from the Contacts component, open the desired Contact window, right-click the e-mail address, and choose Add To Personal Address Book from the object menu.

5. Select your e-mail entry from the list, click the To button to add your e-mail address to the Message Recipients box, and click OK to close the dialog box and redisplay the Message window with your name entered in the To box.

6. Fill in the Subject box, type a message to yourself, and then click the Send button. (If you are not logged on to your e-mail server, Outbox now contains two messages to be sent.)

Attaching Files to Messages

With Outlook, we can send files with our messages. For example, suppose we want to send a letter created in Word to a colleague. The following steps, which use your own e-mail address instead of a colleague's, demonstrate the process:

1. With Inbox active, click the New Mail Message button and then either type your e-mail address in the To edit box or use the To... button to insert the address.

2. In the Subject box, type *Letter sent to Al Pine on January 4, 1998* and press Tab.

3. In the message area, type *Here is the letter I sent to Al regarding the annual report deadline.*

4. Press Enter a couple of times to add some space.

Sending e-mail from the Contacts window

If you want to send an e-mail message to one of your contacts, you can simply right-click the appropriate address card in Contacts and then choose New Message To Contact from the object menu. Outlook displays a Message window with the contact's e-mail address already entered in the To edit box. Complete the other edit boxes in the Message window, type the message, and then click the Send button to send the message.

Converting message headers to contacts

To convert an e-mail message into a contact, drag its header from the Inbox window to the Contacts icon on the Outlook bar. Outlook opens a new Contact window with the complete message displayed. Because of the link between similar fields in Outlook components, Outlook fills in the name and e-mail fields. To fill in the remaining information, you can copy and paste text from the e-mail message to the appropriate fields.

Using virtual business cards (vcards)

You can pass on the information in a contact's card via e-mail with a virtual business card, or vcard. First, display the contents of Contacts, and select the contact. Choose Forward or Forward As Vcard from the Actions menu. Outlook displays a Message window with an icon for the contact. Anyone who opens the message can double-click the icon to display the Contact window or drag the contact icon from the message to the Contacts icon in the Outlook bar.

The Insert File button

5. Click the Insert File button on the toolbar to display the Insert File dialog box shown here:

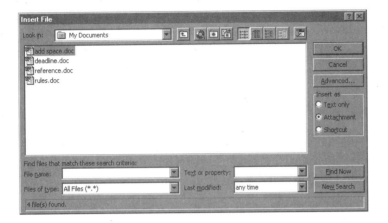

6. Find a short document saved on your hard drive and double-click its filename. Outlook inserts a file icon, as shown here:

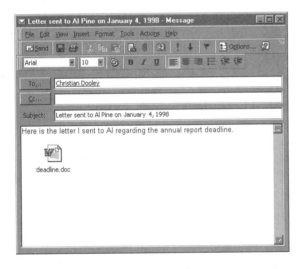

7. Click the Send button.

Sending and Retrieving Messages

If we are connected to our company or Internet e-mail server, we now have three message headers displayed in the workspace. If we aren't connected, we need to log on and send the messages stored in Outbox. We also want to check if we have any mail. Turn the page to see how to send and retrieve messages.

Flagging messages

Flagging messages calls attention to them so that you can be sure an action is carried out. You can flag messages you have received as well as messages you send. To flag a received message so that you can remind yourself to do something with it, simply right-click the message and choose Flag For Follow Up from the object menu. In the Flag To edit box, select an action that needs to be taken, such as Call or Reply. In the Reminder edit box, you can specify a date when you want Outlook to remind you about the flagged message. To flag an outgoing message, choose Flag For Follow Up from the Actions menu in the Message window. Then fill in the Flag To and Reminder edit boxes as necessary and click OK. When the recipient receives the message, Outlook displays the flag symbol next to the message header. When the message is opened, Outlook displays what type of action is requested at the top of the message.

The Send And Receive button

New message alert

1. Click the Send And Receive button on the toolbar. (If Outlook is set up for more than one e-mail service, choose Send And Receive from the Tools menu and then choose the service you want or All Accounts.) Outlook tells you it is checking for new messages and sending outgoing messages. (Internet e-mail users may have to enter a user name and password first.) When Outlook is finished, it displays the number of new messages in parentheses next to the Inbox icon on the Outlook bar, sounds an alert, and displays an envelope icon in the status bar. The message header pane now looks like this:

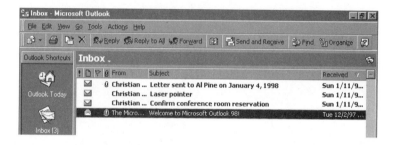

Inbox message symbols

The first column of the Inbox window displays an exclamation mark if the sender has indicated that the message is of high priority. A down arrow indicates that a message is of low priority. (For information on designating the importance level of outgoing messages, see the tip on page 61.) The second column of the Inbox window displays symbols indicating the status of each message. The most common symbols show whether the message has been read—an open envelope—or not—a closed envelope. (For a detailed listing of the other symbols, look up *Inbox, symbols* in online help.) The third column displays a flag symbol if the message has been flagged. (See the tip on the previous page.) The fourth column displays a paper clip icon if the message has an attachment.

Until you read a message, its header in Inbox is displayed in bold type. Icons on the left tell you more about the message (see the adjacent tip). (Notice that Outlook automatically disconnects you from your e-mail server.)

Let's read a message right now:

1. Double-click the header of the message with the letter to Al Pine attachment to display it in a window, like this:

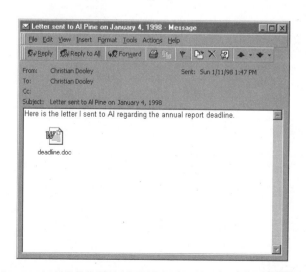

You can also click the message header once to display its contents in the lower half of the workspace. To read the attachment, double-click it. It will open in the program in which it was created.

Replying to Messages

Suppose this message is from a colleague and requires a response. Follow these steps to send a reply:

The Reply button and the Reply To All button

1. Click the Reply button. (To send the response to the sender of the message and to all recipients of courtesy copies, you would click the Reply To All button.) Outlook opens an RE: window like this one:

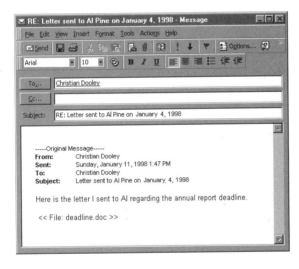

Notice that the To and Subject edit boxes are already filled in. Also notice that the original message appears below the blinking insertion point. (If you prefer not to display the original message in your responses, read the adjacent tip.)

2. Type *Thanks for the letter. That should work!!* Click the Send button to either send the message or to transfer it to Outbox.

Forwarding Messages

If we receive a message that we think will be of interest to a colleague, we can forward the message with a few mouse clicks. Follow the steps on the next page to try it.

No original message in replies

If you don't want Outlook to display the original message at the end of your reply, choose Options from Inbox's Tools menu and click the E-mail Options button on the Preferences tab. Click the arrow to the right of the When Replying To A Message box, select Do Not Include Original Message, and click OK twice. (Notice also that you can change the way the original message appears within a forwarded message using this dialog box.)

The Forward button

1. With the Letter Sent To Al Pine message still displayed in its window, click the Forward button on the toolbar to display the FW: window, as shown here:

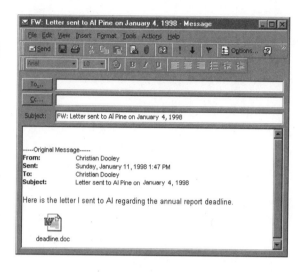

Saving messages and attachments

To save a message for use in another program, select the message in the Inbox window, choose Save As from the File menu, navigate to the desired storage location, name the file, and designate the file type. You can save e-mail messages as RTF Text Format, Text Only, Outlook Template, and Message Format. (The Outlook Template type allows you to use the file as a template for other Outlook messages.The Message Format file type is associated with Outlook, which opens the file if you double-click its filename.) To then save an attachment to an e-mail message as a separate file, open the message, choose Save Attachments from the File menu, and choose the attachment's filename. Then designate the storage location of the file. You can also right-click the attachment icon and choose Save As from the object menu; or you can click the paperclip icon at the right end of the preview pane's title bar and select the file to open it in the appropriate application, where you can save it in the usual way. To save an attachment without opening the message, simply select the message header in the workspace and choose Save Attachments from the File menu.

2. For demonstration purposes, type your own e-mail address in the To box and click the Send button.

3. To view the two new messages, close the message window and if necessary, click the Send And Receive button. Then open each new message once Outlook has retrieved them from your e-mail server.

Deleting Messages

In the early days of e-mail, people would often hold onto old e-mail messages so that they had a record of their senders' addresses. Because it is so easy to add e-mail addresses to the Contacts list, this reason for keeping old messages no longer exists, and after we have read most of our messages, we will probably want to delete them. To demonstrate how to delete messages, we'll clean up the Sent Items folder, but bear in mind that the procedure is the same for any Outlook e-mail folder. Follow the steps at the top of the facing page.

1. Click My Shortcuts and then click the Sent Items icon on the Outlook bar to display a listing in the workspace on the right of all the messages you have sent, as shown here:

The Sent Items icon

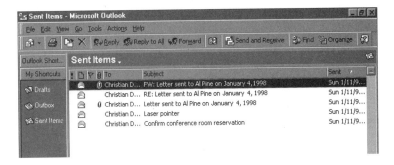

2. Choose Select All from the Edit menu and then click the Delete button on the toolbar. Instead of actually deleting the messages, Outlook transfers them to the Deleted Items folder, giving you another opportunity to change your mind about deleting them.

The Deleted Items icon

3. Click Outlook Shortcuts and then the Deleted Items icon on the Outlook bar to display that folder's contents.

4. You really do want to delete these files, so choose Empty "Deleted Items" Folder from the Tools menu and click Yes in the message box to get rid of the items for good.

5. Display the contents of Inbox and delete all but the five messages you have sent to yourself.

If we want to permanently delete messages and other items without having to later deal with them in the Deleted Items folder, we can choose Options from the Tools menu and select the Empty The Deleted Items Folder Upon Exiting check box in the General section of the Other tab so that Outlook erases the folder's contents every time we exit the program.

Organizing Messages

If we start sending and receiving lots of e-mail messages that we need to keep, we will want to organize Inbox so that specific messages are easier to find. As with the Notes and Contacts components, we can change the way we view messages,

Don't save sent messages

To keep your Outlook files from growing too big, you can turn off the option that automatically saves a copy of all your outgoing messages in the Sent Items folder. Choose Options from the Tools menu, and click the E-mail Options button on the Preferences tab. Deselect the Save Copies Of Messages In Sent Items Folder check box in the Message Handling section and click OK twice. If you later want to save a particular outgoing message in the Sent Items folder, click the Options button in the Message window before you send the message, select the Save Sent Message To check box, designate a location, and click Close.

either by using one of Outlook's predefined views or by creating a view of our own. We can also create folders to supplement the default e-mail folders. For the remainder of this chapter, we will look at ways to keep the messages we send and receive in a more logical order.

Switching Views

So far, we have worked with Inbox using the default Messages view. Let's quickly take a look at some of the other available views:

1. Choose Current View and By Sender from the View menu. The Inbox window looks something like this:

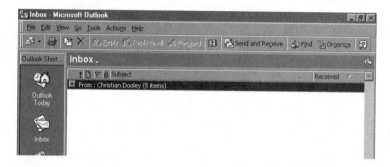

Outlook organizes the messages by sender and displays a plus sign next to each name. When you click the plus sign, Outlook displays all messages from the sender in date/time order, with the most recent message first.

2. Click the plus sign next to your name to display all the messages you have sent to yourself.

3. Click the minus sign to collapse the list again.

4. Now choose Unread Messages from the Current View submenu. In this view, Outlook displays only the messages you have not yet read. (If you have read all of them, the window is blank.)

5. Experiment with some of the other available views and then return to the original view by choosing Messages from the Current View submenu.

Recalling messages

If you are working on a network that uses Exchange Server, you can recall or replace e-mail messages you have recently sent to a coworker. First, display the Sent Items folder and open the message you want to recall. Choose Recall This Message from the Actions menu, select Delete Unread Copies Of This Message, and click OK. To replace the message with a new one, select the second option in the Recall This Message dialog box, click OK, and type a new message. If you want to be notified about the recall or replacement of the message, click the Tell Me check box. (Bear in mind that this feature only works if the recipient has not yet opened or moved the message you want to recall.)

Applying Custom Filters

In the previous section, Outlook displayed only unread messages by applying a *filter* to the list of messages. Filters can help us find a particular message by allowing us to temporarily focus on a subset of the information in the message list. When we want to find a specific message, we can use Outlook's Filter command to create our own filter. Let's look for the message that we received some time during the last seven days about a letter:

1. Choose Current View and then Customize Current View from the View menu to display the View Summary dialog box shown earlier on page 20.

2. Click the Filter button to display this dialog box:

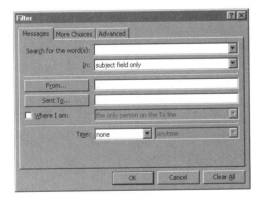

3. On the Messages tab, type *letter* in the Search For The Word(s) edit box.

4. Check that Subject Field Only is selected in the In box to limit the search to the Subject lines of the messages in Inbox, and then type your name in the From box.

5. Click the arrow to the right of the Time box and select Received. Then click the arrow to the right of the adjacent Time box and select In The Last 7 Days.

6. Click OK twice. Outlook filters the message list according to your criteria and displays the results in the workspace as shown on the next page.

More about filters

If you receive tons of messages and need to search for a particular one, you may want to experiment with the other tabs in the Filter dialog box. On the More Choices tab, you can create a filter that looks for messages assigned to a particular category (see page 12 for more information about assigning items to categories), messages that have been read or not, messages that have attachments or not, and ones that have a designated importance level. On the Advanced tab, you can select from several fields by clicking the Field button and selecting a message field from the drop-down list. You can then determine what condition the field must meet by selecting an item from the Condition box. Next, type a value for the field in the Value edit box and click Add To List to add this criteria to the others you have selected. When you click OK twice, Outlook filters your message list and displays only those messages that meet the criteria specified in the Filter dialog box.

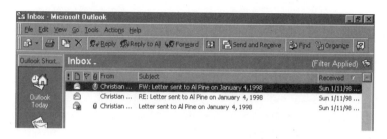

Notice that Outlook displays *(Filter Applied)* at the right end of the workspace title bar to remind you that you are not looking at the complete list of messages.

Removing a filter

7. To redisplay the entire message list, right-click a column header, choose Customize Current View from the object menu, click the Filter button, click Clear All, and then click OK twice.

Using Folders

Switching views and customizing them with filters are two useful ways to organize e-mail. But if we work on many projects simultaneously, we may find that we want to store our e-mail by project. By creating folders to store messages, we can categorize them and keep them better organized. As an example, at Ferguson and Bardell, we might deal with both coworkers and clients. Let's create folders for these two categories now:

1. With Inbox active, choose Folder and then New Folder from the File menu to display this dialog box:

Filtering junk e-mail

Some businesses and organizations send mass mailings via e-mail just as they do via regular mail. If you don't want to receive this junk e-mail, you can tell Outlook to automatically delete it, to move it to a folder other than Inbox, or to color-code it. Display Inbox and click the Organize button on the toolbar. Click the Junk E-Mail option and then select the desired options from the adjacent drop-down lists. After you make your selections, click the Turn On buttons. To designate a specific address as junk e-mail, right-click the message header and choose Junk E-Mail and then Add To Junk Senders List from the object menu. (You can filter e-mail messages with adult content in the same way.)

2. Type *Coworkers* in the Name box and click OK. Outlook displays this message box:

3. Click Yes and notice that the My Shortcuts button flashes on the Outlook bar.

4. Click the My Shortcuts button to see the new icon for the Co-workers folder.

5. Repeat steps 1 through 3 to create a folder called *Clients*.

   If we create several new folders, the Outlook bar begins to fill up and scrolling to find a particular folder takes more effort. To see more folder icons at a glance, we can display the folders as a list, like this:

1. Choose Folder List from the View menu. The Outlook window now looks like this:

Displaying the folder list

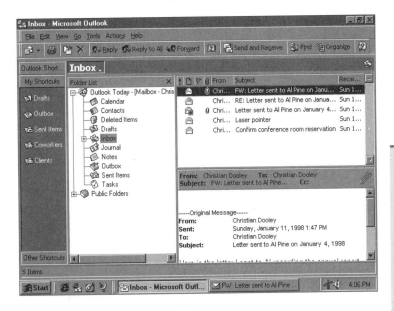

Quickly displaying the folder list

To quickly display the folder list without leaving it on, you can click the arrow to the right of the component name in the workspace title bar to display the folder list. If you decide to keep the folder list displayed, simply click the push pin in the top right corner of the list.

As you can see, the folder list is sandwiched between the Outlook bar and the workspace.

2. In the list, click the plus sign next to the Inbox folder to display the folders you just created.

3. To display only the folder list, choose Outlook Bar from the View menu to turn it off.

Moving Messages

We have created a couple of folders in which to place our messages, so now we need to move the messages into the appropriate storage locations. Follow these steps:

1. With the Inbox folder selected in the folder list and its contents displayed in the workspace, select all three messages about the letter to Al Pine by selecting one, holding down the Shift key, and selecting the last one.

2. With the messages highlighted, drag them to the Clients folder. When you release the mouse button, Outlook moves the messages from the Inbox folder to the Clients folder.

3. Next, move one of the other messages from the Inbox folder to the Coworkers folder.

Faxing

In addition to e-mail, Outlook can handle faxes. If you are working on a stand-alone computer, the Internet Support version of Outlook 98 includes Outlook Fax. If you are working on a network and have Microsoft Fax installed on your computer, the Corporate Support version of Outlook 98 updates your fax capabilities for use with Outlook. (If Microsoft Fax is not installed, you must first install it by accessing the Windows Setup tab of the Add/Remove Programs dialog box. Then install the fax update from Add Components on the Outlook installation CD-ROM.) To send a fax, choose New Fax Message from the Actions menu in the Inbox window or the Contacts window. Outlook opens the Fax Wizard which guides you through the process of creating the fax. Before you can receive a fax, you have some setup work to complete in Outlook. From Inbox, choose Microsoft Fax Tools and then Options from the Tools menu. Display the Modem tab and click the Properties button. Change the Answer Mode property to either Manual or Automatically Answer to answer after a specified number of rings. When you select the Manual option, you need to click the Answer button on your screen when someone sends you a fax. When Outlook receives a fax, it puts it in the Inbox folder, like an e-mail message. You can then open, move, and delete the fax, just like an e-mail message.

4. Click the Folder List's Close button to close it and then choose Outlook Bar from the View menu to redisplay the Outlook bar.

Closing the folder list

Well, that wraps up our discussion of the e-mail component of Outlook. Keeping your messages organized efficiently is bound to make you more productive, so we encourage you to experiment with the organization features discussed in this and the other chapters.

Managing Your Schedule

4

In this chapter, we show you how to use Outlook's Calendar component to manage your time. We schedule appointments, set up a recurring appointment, and allocate time for day-long and week-long events. Then we see how to use Calendar to plan meetings and send out meeting requests to attendees.

*Check the schedules
of coworkers to
plan a meeting*

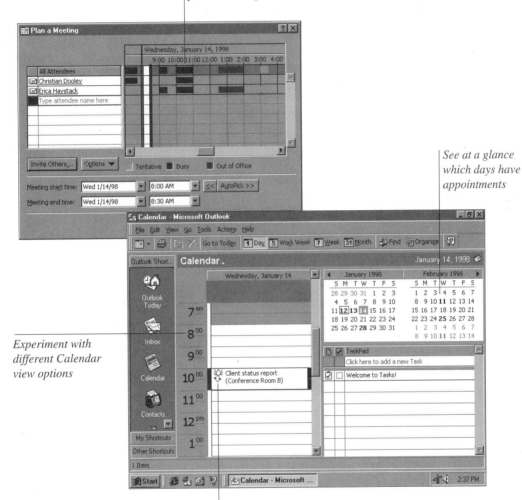

*See at a glance
which days have
appointments*

*Experiment with
different Calendar
view options*

*Enter onetime and
recurring appointments
in the Calendar*

The Calendar component of Outlook is designed to take the hassle out of time management by enabling us to keep track of appointments. If used faithfully, Calendar can eliminate the need for a paper calendar and can actually function better than one. With Calendar, we can create detailed appointments, set recurring appointments, plan meetings, and ask to be reminded of these commitments ahead of time.

Outlook's Calendar component is most useful when we keep Outlook running throughout the workday. Some of the features are available only if we are working on a network where Microsoft Exchange Server handles internal communications. In this chapter, we'll explore all of Calendar's useful features. If your network doesn't use Exchange Server, you can skip the sections that don't apply for your computer's setup. Let's take a look at Calendar now:

The Calendar icon

1. After starting Outlook, click the Calendar icon on the Outlook bar. The workspace now looks like this:

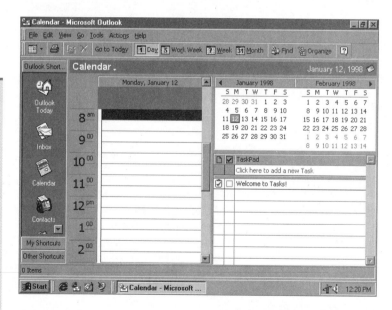

Computer date and time

Outlook obtains the date and time from your system clock. If this clock is wrong, Outlook keeps an inaccurate calendar and reminds you of appointments at the wrong time. To set the correct date and time, double-click the clock at the right end of the Windows taskbar to display the Date/Time Properties dialog box. Then make the appropriate adjustments to the date or time. If Outlook has trouble keeping your schedule, there may be problems with your computer's battery, which maintains the system clock.

On the left side is the *appointment area*, divided into half-hour intervals. In the top right corner is the Date Navigator, which displays calendars for the current month and next month. (You can cycle through the months by clicking the left and right arrows on the calendar headers.) In the bottom right corner is a small version of the Tasks window, where you keep your to-do list. (We discuss the Tasks component and the to-do list in Chapter 5.) By default, Outlook displays the calendar for today.

Scheduling Appointments

The half-hour intervals in the appointment area designate *time slots*. We use these time slots to schedule appointments for the day. Suppose we have a meeting with Al Pine at 3:00 this afternoon. We expect the meeting to last half an hour. Let's enter the appointment:

1. Scroll the appointment area, click the 3:00 time slot, type *Al Pine*, and press Enter. (If it is now later than 3:00 PM, pick a later time. You can enter an appointment that has already occurred, but you can't set a reminder.)

Entering appointments directly

That's all there is to it. Today's date is now bold in the Date Navigator, indicating that you have an appointment today. (If you are working on a network that uses Exchange Server, by default the time slot holding the appointment indicates to anyone viewing your schedule that you are unavailable during that time.)

Now suppose we need to schedule an interview with a prospective new financial analyst named Dolly Bills at 4:15 PM tomorrow. The interview will probably last an hour and a half. Follow these steps:

1. Click tomorrow's date in the Date Navigator. Tomorrow's appointment area is now displayed.

2. Because the Calendar time slots are in half-hour intervals, you need to make a special entry for Dolly Bills. Double-click the 4:00 time slot to display the Appointment window shown on the next page, in which you can tailor your appointments.

Other methods for entering appointments

Another way to add an appointment to your schedule is to select the complete time of the appointment with the mouse, right-click the selection, and choose New Appointment from the object menu. Outlook then displays the Appointment window with the start and end times already filled in. If you don't want to enter appointments directly from the appointment area, you can instead click the New Appointment button on the toolbar or choose New and then Appointment from the File menu to display the Appointment window.

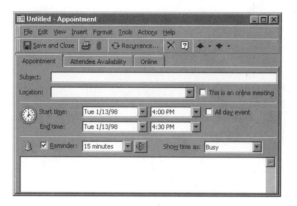

3. If necessary, maximize the window.

4. In the Subject edit box, type *Dolly Bills*, and in the Location edit box, type *Conference Room B*. (You can also click the arrow to the right of the Location edit box to select from a drop-down list of the last seven locations you have used.)

Tailoring the start time ➤ 5. To change the start time, select 00 in 4:00 PM, and type *15*. Then change the end time to 5:45 PM by clicking the arrow to the right of the End Time edit box and selecting 5:45 from the drop-down list.

6. If necessary, click the Reminder check box to select it, and then change the amount of warning time from 15 minutes to 10 minutes by either typing the time or selecting it from the drop-down list.

7. Click the arrow to the right of the Show Time As edit box to display a drop-down list of four options: Free, Tentative, Busy, and Out Of Office. If you are working on a network that uses Exchange Server, these four options show anyone who is trying to set up a meeting whether or not you are available at this time. Selecting Tentative or Free displays the time in light blue or white on other people's computers and indicates that you might be available. Selecting Busy or Out Of Office displays the time in dark blue or purple and indicates that you are not available.

8. Leave the Busy option selected, and then click the Private check box in the bottom right corner of the window. (Other

Using AutoCreate

Outlook's AutoCreate feature allows you to create appointments based on e-mail messages you have received. To use Auto-Create, select the desired message header in Inbox and drag it to the Calendar icon on the Outlook bar. Outlook then displays the Appointment window with the contents of the message displayed in the message area at the bottom of the window and with the message subject displayed in the Subject edit box. To complete the appointment, fill in the remaining information and then click Save And Close.

people will see that you are not available at this time, but they will not be able to see why.)

9. Click Save And Close to confirm the appointment. The Calendar window now looks like this:

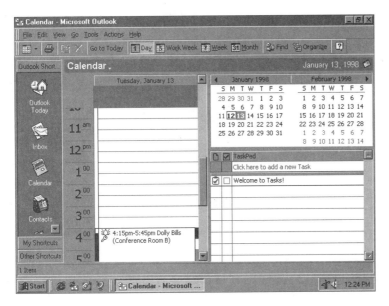

10. Click the Go To Today button on the toolbar or click today's date in the Date Navigator to move back to the appointment area for today.

When the reminder time for the appointment arrives, Outlook displays this dialog box:

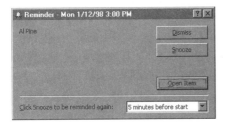

We can click the Dismiss button to tell Outlook not to remind us again about this appointment. We can designate another reminder time using the drop-down list at the bottom of the dialog box and then click the Snooze button. Or we can click the

Changing workday default times

By default, Outlook uses an 8:00 AM to 5:00 PM, Monday through Friday workweek and displays these hours in the appointment area in white with all other hours of the day dimmed. But if your schedule is different, you can change the default times and days. Choose Options from the Tools menu and click the Calendar Options button on the Preferences tab. In the Calendar Work Week section, enter the start and end times of your workday. To change the days worked, click the desired days' check boxes. Then click OK twice.

Open Item button to display the Appointment window and refresh our memory about the details of the appointment.

Scheduling Recurring Appointments

Unless we specify otherwise, the appointments we schedule are onetime occurrences. We can designate appointments that occur at the same time at regular intervals as *recurring*. Then instead of having to enter the appointment manually over and over again, we can let Outlook automatically make that appointment for us.

For example, suppose we meet with a group of senior consultants every other Wednesday from 10:00 to 11:00 AM. Here's how to schedule this recurring appointment:

1. Click next Wednesday's date in the Date Navigator and drag through the time slots from 10:00 to 11:00 to select them.

2. Choose New Recurring Appointment from the Actions menu to display this dialog box:

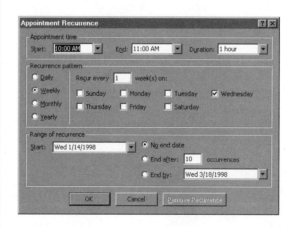

By default, Outlook assumes you want the meeting to occur weekly on the same day of the week, starting and ending at the times you selected, with no end date.

3. In the Recurrence Pattern section, enter 2 in the Recur Every edit box to change the appointment to every other week.

Inserting files in appointments

If a file is associated with an appointment you have scheduled, you can attach the file to the appointment—for example, to remind you to print it beforehand. After scheduling the appointment in the Appointment window, click an insertion point in the message area at the bottom of the window and click the Insert File button on the toolbar. Outlook displays the Insert File dialog box shown earlier on page 65, where you navigate to the file you want to attach and select it. You can then specify how you want the file inserted by selecting an option in the Insert As section. If you insert the file as text, the file becomes part of the appointment. If you insert the file as an attachment, Outlook attaches a copy of the file to the appointment as an icon. You can then make changes to the copy without affecting the original, and vice versa. If you insert the file as a shortcut, Outlook adds a shortcut in the appointment that you can double-click to open the original file. Once you make your Insert As selection, click OK to insert the file according to your specifications.

4. To add an end date, click the End By option in the Range Of Recurrence section and use the drop-down calendar to change the date to *December 2, 1998*. Then click OK.

Specifying an end date for a recurring appointment

5. In the Appointment window, type *Client status report* in the Subject edit box. Click the arrow to the right of the Location edit box and select Conference Room B, change the reminder time for the appointment to 30 minutes, and then click Save And Close. The result is shown here:

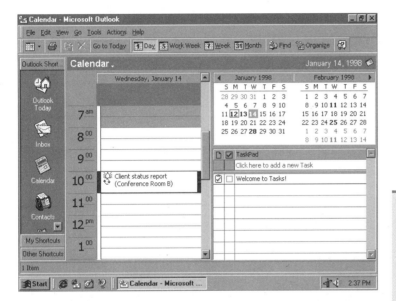

Outlook has entered the recurring appointment in the specified time slot for next Wednesday and for every other Wednesday thereafter, designating it with circular arrows to indicate that the appointment is recurring.

Scheduling Events

Sometimes appointments last for an entire day or even longer. Outlook refers to these long appointments as *events*. For example, we might need to schedule a day-long presentation at a client's office or attend a week-long conference in another city. Scheduling events is similar to scheduling regular appointments. Here's what you do:

1. Click a date two weeks from now on the Date Navigator, and double-click the blank space at the top of the appointment

Problems with the Every Weekday option?

If you altered your workday settings (see the tip on page 81), Outlook doesn't record recurring appointments correctly when you use the Every Weekday option in the Recurrence Pattern section of the Appointment Recurrence dialog box. (This option becomes available after you click the Daily option.) For example, if you have set your workdays to Tuesday through Saturday and then you create a recurring appointment for every weekday, Outlook schedules the appointment for the default Monday through Friday week. To work around this problem, use the Weekly option instead of the Every Weekday option and then select the check boxes for the desired days.

area to tell Outlook that you want to enter an event. Outlook displays this Event window:

2. Type *Annual Report Presentation* in the Subject edit box, type *Sweet Forgiveness Corporate Office* in the Location edit box, change the Reminder setting to 0.5 days, and change the Show Time As option to Out Of Office. Notice that Outlook has selected the All Day Event check box.

3. Click Save And Close to display the event in the appointment area, like this:

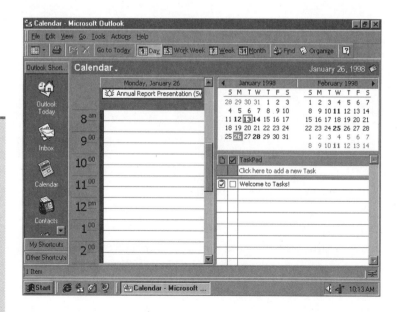

Making existing appointments recur

To turn an existing appointment into a recurring one, double-click the appointment in the appointment area and choose Recurrence from the Actions menu. Outlook displays the Appointment Recurrence dialog box, where you can select the recurrence options you want. When you finish, click OK and then click Save And Close.

Now suppose we want to enter a week-long event for a conference we will attend in Boston. Follow these steps:

1. Click the Monday following the presentation at Sweet Forgiveness in the Date Navigator, and then choose New All Day Event from the Actions menu to display the Event window.

Entering week-long events

2. Type *Boston Financial Conference* in the Subject edit box, type *Charles River Convention Center* in the Location edit box, and change the Show Time As option to Out Of Office.

3. Click the arrow to the right of the End Time edit box and block out the entire week by selecting the Friday of the week you have chosen. Outlook may display a warning message at the top of the window stating that you already have another appointment entered during this time (the recurring senior consultant's meeting).

4. Go ahead and click Save And Close.

5. Notice in the Date Navigator that the entire week is now marked in bold. Click one or two of the dates in the designated week to check that Outlook has entered the conference correctly.

Editing Appointments

Sometimes we will need to change an appointment to either fix errors or update details. Usually, we can double-click the appointment to open its Appointment window and then edit the appropriate area, but for certain changes we can take shortcuts. Let's try some shortcuts now as we change the appointment time for the interview with Dolly Bills:

1. First, display the calendar for the day on which you entered Dolly Bill's interview appointment.

2. Point to the blue border on the left side of the appointment, and when the pointer turns into a four-headed arrow, hold down the left mouse button and drag upward to the 3:00 PM time slot.

Scheduling recurring events

Like appointments, events can occur regularly at weekly, monthly, or yearly intervals. For example, if you always have a day-long meeting at a client's office on the last Friday of every month or if your office always closes the day after Thanksgiving, you can mark these recurring events throughout your calendar. First, choose New All Day Event from the Actions menu to display the Appointment window. Then choose Recurrence from the Actions menu and notice that the start and end times are set to Midnight, designating the appointment as an all day event. Fill in the information as you would with any other appointment, click OK, and then click Save And Close. Bear in mind that when you enter recurring events such as birthdays and anniversaries in a contact's address card, the event is automatically added to the calendar. (See page 38 for more information.)

3. When the top of the appointment box is even with the 3:00 PM time slot, release the mouse button. Outlook moves the appointment and adjusts the times displayed in the box to reflect the fact that the appointment starts at the quarter-hour, as shown here:

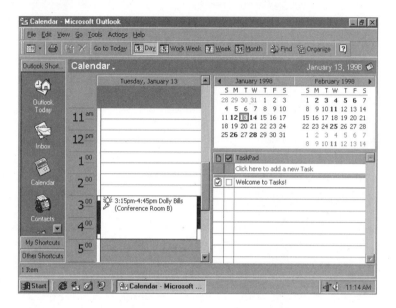

Now suppose we need to allow an additional half-hour for Al Pine's appointment. Here's how to change the appointment in the appointment area:

1. Display the Al Pine appointment and point to the bottom border of its time slot.

2. When the pointer turns into a double-headed arrow, drag downward to the 4:00 PM marker and then release the mouse button. The appointment is now scheduled for a full hour.

If we need to change an appointment to a different date, we can accomplish this task in the appointment area as well. Let's move Al Pine's appointment to the day after tomorrow (or the next working day, if tomorrow is a Saturday or Sunday):

1. Point to the Al Pine appointment and drag it to the correct date on the Date Navigator.

Adding holidays

If you work with clients or customers in other countries, you may want to track the national holidays of those countries in Calendar. To do so, choose Options from the Tools menu, click Calendar Options on the Preferences tab, and then click the Add Holidays button. You can then select the holidays of various countries as well as those of certain religions to add them to your calendar.

2. Release the mouse button. Outlook displays the calendar for the new date and enters the appointment in the same time slot.

Editing Recurring Appointments

Editing a recurring appointment works pretty much the same way as editing any other type of appointment, except that Outlook gives you the option of changing just one occurrence of the appointment or all of them. Suppose the next client status meeting, which occurs every other Wednesday, will take place in Conference Room A instead of Conference Room B. Follow these steps to change the location of this particular meeting:

1. Click the date of the next client status meeting, and then double-click its box. Outlook displays this message box:

← Editing one occurrence

2. We want to change only this occurrence, so check that the Open This Occurrence option is selected and click OK.

3. When Outlook displays the Appointment window, change Conference Room B to *Conference Room A* in the Location edit box and click Save And Close.

Canceling Appointments

In addition to editing appointments, we will sometimes need to delete them altogether. Suppose Al Pine has called to cancel his meeting. Follow these steps to delete the appointment from Calendar:

1. Display the Al Pine appointment and click it once to select it.

2. Click the Delete button on the toolbar. Outlook instantly removes the appointment. (If you delete an appointment by mistake, you can choose Undo Delete from the Edit menu to move it back to the appointment area.)

Using AutoDate

In date and time fields, you can type a description of the desired date or time in words and Outlook will quickly convert the phrase to the correct number format using a process called AutoDate. For example, if on the tenth of January you type *one week from tomorrow*, Outlook will display January 18th for the date. You can also spell out times, such as *noon* or *midnight*, and use holidays that fall on the same date every year, such as *Christmas* or *Halloween*.

The procedure for canceling a recurring appointment is much the same as the one for canceling an individual appointment, except that we must decide whether to delete one occurrence of the appointment or all occurrences. We can also convert a recurring appointment to a onetime event. Suppose the senior consultants have decided that after the next client status meeting, client reports will be added to the agenda of the weekly staff meeting instead of being addressed separately. Here's how to make this change:

Canceling recurring appointments

1. Move to the first appointment of the recurring series and double-click it to display the message box shown on the previous page.

2. Select the Open The Series option and click OK.

3. In the Recurring Appointment window, click the Recurrence button to display the Appointment Recurrence dialog box.

4. Click the Remove Recurrence button.

5. Outlook has changed the Location setting to Conference Room B, so reselect Conference Room A from the Location dropdown list and then click Save And Close in the Appointment window.

By the way, you cannot undo this operation. The only way to restore the recurring appointment is to display its Appointment window, click the Recurrence button, and reenter its information.

Finding Appointments

As our calendar begins to fill up, we may find it increasingly difficult to locate a particular appointment, meeting, or event. If we have a good idea of what we're looking for, we can use the Find button. Follow these steps:

The Find button

1. With Calendar displayed, click the Find button on the toolbar to display a Find area at the top of the workspace, as shown on the facing page.

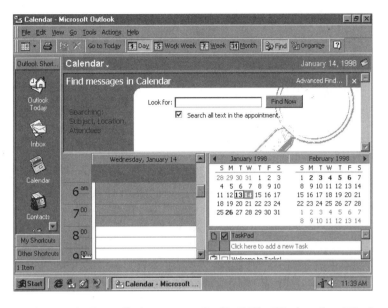

2. In the Look For edit box, type *Dolly Bills*. Notice that Find states it will look for words in the Subject, Location, and Attendees fields.

3. Click Find Now. Outlook looks for an appointment that contains the specified words and displays the results at the bottom of the workspace in the Active Appointments table view (with a filter applied to the Subject column), as shown here:

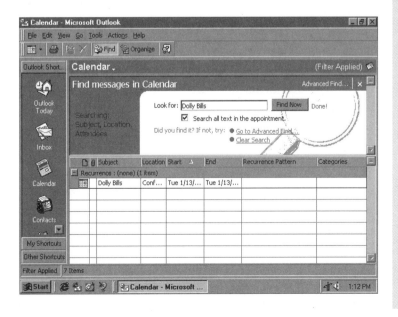

More complex searches

You can carry out more complex searches in the Find area by clicking Advanced Find. Outlook displays an Advanced Find dialog box very similar to the Filter dialog box shown earlier on page 71. On the Appointments And Meetings tab, you can enter more search criteria. By default, Find searches the currently active Outlook component, but you can change the component by selecting a different option from the Look For drop-down list. The More Choices and Advanced tabs of the Advanced Find dialog box work the same way as they do in the Filter dialog box. (See the tip on page 71 for more information.) Once you finish entering your search criteria, click Find Now to begin the search.

If your search is unsuccessful, you can click Go To Advanced Find (see the tip on the previous page) to refine the search, or you can click Clear Search to begin again.

4. Click the Find area's Close button to exit and return Calendar to its default view.

Planning a Meeting

The advent of programs such as Microsoft NetMeeting (see page 157) means that we no longer have to be physically present at a meeting to be able to participate. (As we describe in Chapter 7, we can use NetMeeting to set up audio- and video-conferences, collaborate on projects, share files, and have on-screen "chat" sessions via the Internet.) Nevertheless, the face-to-face meeting is still the most common means of collective communication in the workplace. Whether a meeting is electronic or face-to-face, it needs to be scheduled. If we are working on a network that uses Exchange Server, we can use electronic communication to take some of the hassle out of setting up meetings. With the help of Outlook's Calendar component, we can check other people's calendars to determine an appropriate time and place for a meeting and send out meeting requests to potential attendees, without the back-and-forth usually involved in such a task.

Sending Meeting Requests

Suppose we want to set up a meeting for next Wednesday. For this example, we will coordinate schedules and send out a meeting request to just one person, but you will easily be able to see how the procedure could be applied to several meeting attendees. (If you are not working on a network that uses Exchange Server, simply read along so that you can get an idea of the procedure.) Let's get started:

Selecting a meeting time

1. With Calendar's contents displayed in the workspace, choose Plan A Meeting from the Actions menu. Outlook then opens the Plan A Meeting dialog box, as shown at the top of the facing page.

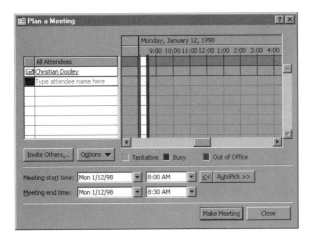

The timeline on the right side of the dialog box displays today's date, showing any appointments scheduled for today blocked out with colored lines representing the type of appointment (see page 80).

2. To schedule a meeting for next Wednesday, use the horizontal scroll bars to scroll that day's schedule into view.

3. To invite someone to attend the meeting, click the Invite Others button. Outlook displays this dialog box, with your name already entered in the Required box:

Selecting attendees

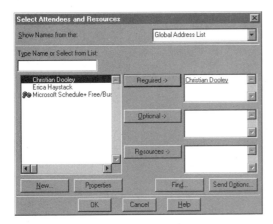

You can change the setting in the Show Names From The box to display the contents of a different address book. (See page 53 for more information about address books.)

Other ways of requesting meetings

You can also create a meeting request by choosing New Meeting Request from the Actions menu. Instead of displaying the Plan A Meeting dialog box, Outlook displays the Meeting window. You then fill in the information as you would normally. To invite people to the meeting and to check their schedules using this method, use the window's Attendee Availability tab.

4. Select the name of the person you want to invite from the address book list, click the Required button, and click OK. (If you want to invite someone to the meeting whose presence is desired but not necessary, select his or her name from the address book list, click the Optional button, and click OK.) Outlook adds a row to the timeline displaying the schedule of the person you want to invite, like this:

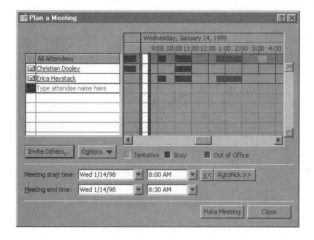

Notice that Outlook uses a white bar to highlight the first half-hour time slot available for all attendees.

5. Click the AutoPick >> button to move to the next available time slot, and then either continue clicking until the white bar sits at the slot you want or simply click the desired slot.

Sending meeting requests →

6. To send a meeting request to the person you selected, first click the Make Meeting button. Outlook displays a modified Appointment window, like this one:

Online meetings

To hold a meeting online over the Internet or an intranet, click the This Is An Online Meeting check box on the Appointment tab of the Meeting window. By default, Outlook uses NetMeeting for online meetings (see page 157). You can specify the type and location of the online meeting on the Online tab of the Meeting window.

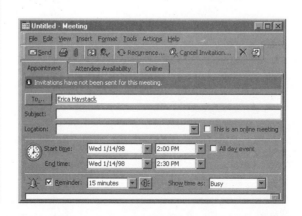

7. Notice that the selected person's e-mail address is in the To edit box. For purposes of demonstration, replace this e-mail address with your own.

8. Type *Client Update Meeting* in the Subject edit box and select Conference Room B from the Location drop-down list. Then change the time in the End Time edit box so that the meeting will last one hour.

9. Click an insertion point in the blank note area and type *Hope this time will work for you*. (You may need to maximize the window to display this section.)

10. Finally, click the Send button. Outlook sends an e-mail message to the designated address, requesting the meeting at the specified time.

Editing Meeting Requests

Sometimes we may need to add or remove attendees from a meeting request or we may need to change another piece of information, such as the location. Let's edit the meeting we just scheduled:

1. Locate the client update meeting in the appointment area and double-click its box to display the Meeting window.

2. Change the location to Conference Room A.

3. Click the Attendee Availability tab to display the information shown here:

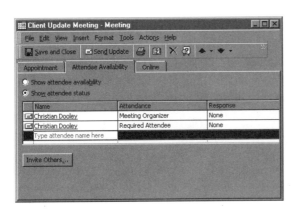

Creating recurring meetings

To create a new recurring meeting, first choose New Recurring Meeting from the Actions menu. Fill in the Appointment Recurrence dialog box as usual and click OK. Next, fill in the necessary information on the Appointment and Attendee Availability tabs and click Send. To turn an existing meeting into a recurring one, first open the meeting by double-clicking its box in the appointment area. Then click the Recurrence button to display the Appointment Recurrence dialog box. Fill in the information as usual and then click OK. In the Recurring Meeting window, click the Send Update button so that you can notify all participants of the change.

Your name appears as both Meeting Organizer and Required Attendee because you changed the e-mail address in step 7 on the previous page. Usually you will see a list of the people whose names you selected in the Select Attendees And Resources dialog box (see page 91). To add or remove attendees, you can click the Invite Others button, add or remove the appropriate people, and then click OK. (Don't make any attendee changes now.)

Adding or removing meeting attendees

4. To notify the attendees of the location change, click the Send Update button on the toolbar. Outlook sends a new e-mail message to the meeting attendee (in this case, you) and closes the Meeting window.

Responding to Meeting Requests

Now that we know how to request a meeting, we need to see how things work on the receiving end. Because we sent the meeting request to ourselves, follow these steps to check for the meeting request:

1. Display the contents of Inbox in the workspace and, if needed, click the Send and Receive button to check for new messages.

2. Once you receive the messages regarding the meeting, open the first meeting request you sent, which displays a message stating the request is out-of-date. (Outlook adds this notification because the meeting request has been updated.)

3. Close the window and then open the second message, which looks like this:

Canceling meetings

If you need to cancel a meeting, first open the meeting in its Meeting window. Then choose Cancel Meeting from the Actions menu. Outlook displays a message box, giving you the option of deleting the meeting and sending cancellation notices to all attendees or deleting the meeting without sending the cancellation notice. Select the option you want and then click OK. If you are sending cancellation notices, be sure to click the Send button in the Meeting window before closing it. If you receive a meeting cancellation notice, you can click the Remove From Calendar button to remove the meeting from your calendar.

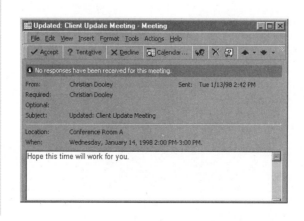

At the top of the window, Outlook displays a message that no responses have been received for the meeting. If a conflict in your schedule means the requested meeting time won't work for you, Outlook also informs you of the conflict. Toolbar buttons provide three options for responding to the meeting request. You can accept, tentatively accept, or decline.

4. Choose Calendar from the View menu to check whether the meeting fits with your schedule, and then close the window.

5. Click the appropriate response button to send your reply to the meeting organizer. In this case, because you are the meeting organizer, Outlook displays a message saying no response is needed. Click OK to close the message box.

6. Close the Meeting window and delete the two meeting requests before moving on. You might also want to cancel the meeting by following the instructions in the tip shown on the facing page.

Customizing Calendar

The Calendar component of Outlook can be altered using the customization features we discussed in earlier chapters. However, we also want to show you different ways we can view schedules in Calendar and some ways of customizing Calendar to make it easier to use.

The first three Calendar views are grouped in one category called *Day/Week/Month*. By default, Calendar displays our schedules in *day view*, meaning it displays the appointment area for one day only, with the times along the left side at half-hour intervals. Let's look at some ways we can customize day view:

1. To change the time interval, right-click any time to display an object menu. Notice that you can choose an interval from 5 to 60 minutes from the bottom section of the menu.

2. Choose 15 minutes from the object menu. Your appointment area now looks like the one shown on the next page.

More Calendar options

In the Calendar Options dialog box, you can set options that relate to meetings. To access this dialog box, choose Options from the Tools menu and click Calendar Options on the Preferences tab. If you click the Resource Scheduling button, you can set options to automatically accept or decline certain types of meeting requests. If you click the Free/Busy Options button, you can enter how many months of your schedule are posted on the network server, as well as how often your schedule gets updated on the server.

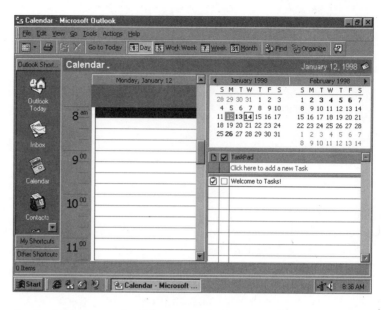

Outlook keeps track of time zone information based on specifications made when Windows was installed on your computer. If necessary, we can change or add a time zone directly in Outlook. Let's add another time zone to the appointment area so that we can keep track of things in the London office of Ferguson and Bardell:

Adding a time zone → 1. Choose Options from the Tools menu, and on the Preferences tab, click the Calendar Options button.

2. Click the Time Zone button in the Calendar Options section. Outlook displays this dialog box:

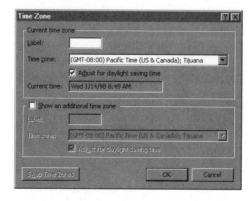

3. In the Label edit box of the Current Time Zone section, type *Seattle*.

4. Next, click the Show An Additional Time Zone check box, type *London* in the Label edit box, select the (GMT) Greenwich Mean Time option from about the middle of the Time Zone drop-down list, and click OK three times. The appointment area now looks like this:

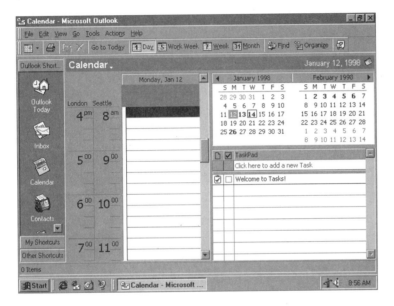

5. To remove the London time zone, right-click the time interval area, choose Change Time Zone from the object menu, and deselect the Show An Additional Time Zone check box. Then delete the Seattle label and click OK.

Removing a time zone

To display more days at once in the appointment area, we can switch to *week view* (seven days) or *work week view* (five days). Or, we can survey the entire month in *month view*. Let's take a look at these views now:

The Week button

1. Click the Week button on the toolbar to change Calendar's display to look like the one at the top of the next page.

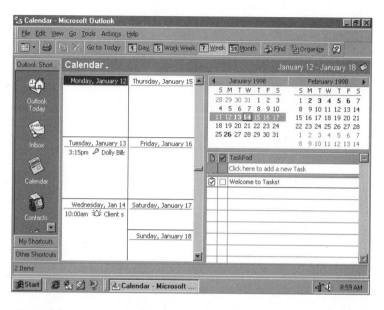

The Date Navigator and TaskPad remain the same, but the appointment area changes to display the appointments for the week. All the information pertaining to each appointment is included except for the color-coded status bars.

The Month button

2. Click the Month button to change Calendar's display to look like this:

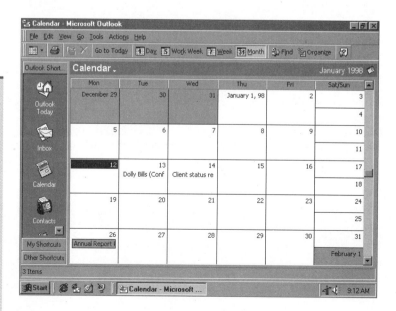

Printing schedules

To print a calendar, choose Print from the File menu or click the Print button on the toolbar. Then select a print layout and any other options you want in the Print dialog box, and click OK. If you're not sure what type of layout you want to print, select one of the layout options and click the Preview button. You can also specify the dates you want to print in the Print Range section of the Print dialog box.

The Date Navigator and TaskPad areas disappear. If not all the appointments for a particular day will fit in the appointment area, Outlook displays a yellow arrow button indicating that information is hidden. Clicking this button displays that day's calendar in day view.

The Day button

3. Click the Day button to return to the default day view with today's date displayed.

Calendar's remaining views are accessible through the Current View submenu on the View menu. Each view (except the By Category view) sorts appointments by recurrence group first and then by chronological order. The By Category view sorts appointments by assigned rather than default categories, so you must assign your appointments to specific categories in order to take advantage of this view. As you experiment with the different views, remember that you can customize them by grouping items or by defining new views.

That wraps up this chapter on the Calendar component of Outlook. Now that you know the ins and outs of using this feature, you'll have no more excuses for forgetting appointments or being late to meetings!

5

Keeping a To-Do List

By using Outlook's Tasks component, we can keep
track of tasks and projects in an electronic to-do
list. In this chapter, we show how to manage and
prioritize tasks, as well as how to delegate them to
other people.

Set due dates and
reminder times for tasks

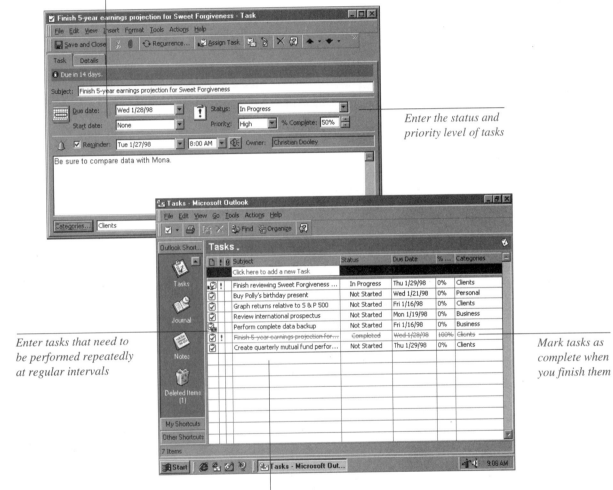

Enter the status and
priority level of tasks

Enter tasks that need to
be performed repeatedly
at regular intervals

Mark tasks as
complete when
you finish them

Experiment with different
views for your to-do list

As our schedules become increasingly busy, we often have trouble juggling the many tasks we need to accomplish during the day. To make matters more complicated, we are often trying to accomplish personal tasks as well as business tasks. In the past, many of us kept track of the things we needed to do either in our heads or on pieces of paper (with varying degrees of legibility). Now we can use Outlook's Tasks component to create efficient, readable, and organized to-do lists.

Using Tasks, not only can we manage and prioritize our work, but if necessary, we can also schedule time for specific tasks in our calendars. If we are working on a network that uses Exchange Server, other people in our company can then check our schedule and see that we are unavailable during the time we plan to work on a task. (For more information, see "Planning a Meeting" on page 90.) In this chapter, we discuss how to create entries and how to deal with our tasks in their various stages. We also show you ways to organize tasks to make the best use of this Outlook component and how to electronically delegate tasks to coworkers.

Adding Tasks

We don't have to do anything to create a to-do list template, but before we can do anything with it, we will need to add some tasks to it. We can add tasks when Calendar is displayed in the Outlook workspace by clicking the new-task area at the top of the TaskPad. But in this chapter, we'll work directly with the Tasks component. We'll start by adding a simple task; then we'll add a task with a deadline and one with high priority. Follow these steps:

The Tasks icon

1. With Outlook started, click the Tasks icon on the Outlook bar to open the empty to-do list shown at the top of the facing page. (You may need to click the down arrow at the bottom of the Outlook bar to see the Tasks icon.)

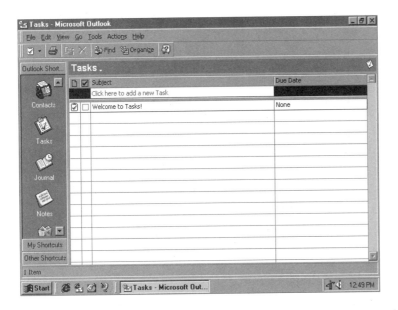

If your to-do list looks different from ours, choose Current View and then Simple List from the View menu. (We discuss other views on page 110.) You see four columns of information:

- **The Icon column.** The icon indicates the type of item. (In most cases, the item will be a regular task.)

- **The Complete column.** If you have designated the task as complete, the box in this column is checked.

- **The Subject column.** This column displays the description entered for the task, such as *Send get-well card to Rocky.*

- **The Due Date column.** If you have set no due date, the column contains the word *None.*

2. Click *Click Here To Add A New Task* in the Subject column, type *Pick up dry cleaning*, click None in the Due Date column, click the down arrow, select tomorrow's date from the drop-down calendar, and press Enter.

Now suppose we want to add an important task that must be completed by tomorrow afternoon. By default, tasks have no due date, have not yet started, and have normal priority. Follow the steps on the next page to enter start and due dates and assign a priority level.

Other ways to add tasks

If you want to add a task while working in another Outlook component, you can click the arrow to the right of the New button and select Task, press Ctrl+Shift+K, or choose New and then Task from the File menu. If you want to add a task without opening Outlook and have installed the Office shortcut bar (see page 8), you can click the New Task button. If you are working in Word, Excel, or PowerPoint, you can create a new task that is automatically linked to the open document. First, display the Reviewing toolbar by right-clicking an open toolbar and choosing Reviewing from the object menu. Then click the Create Microsoft Outlook Task button to display a Task window with the document's name entered in the Subject edit box and a shortcut to the file in the message area of the window.

The New Task button ————————► 1. Click the New Task button to display this window:

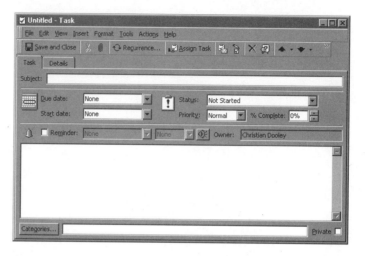

2. Type *Create quarterly mutual fund performance report* in the Subject edit box. Click the arrow to the right of the Due Date edit box, and when the calendar appears, click tomorrow's date. Change the Priority setting to High, and finally, click Save And Close. As you can see here, your two tasks are now listed in the workspace:

Setting a priority level ————————►

Using AutoCreate

If you receive e-mail messages that contain tasks you need to add to your to-do list or if you need to create a task based on an appointment entered in the Calendar, you can use Auto-Create to streamline the process. To convert an e-mail message into a task, select its header in Inbox and drag it to the Tasks icon. Outlook then opens the Task window with the message text displayed in the bottom area. Fill in the remaining information (such as priority and due date) and click Save And Close. To create a task based on an appointment, drag the appointment from the workspace to the Tasks icon. Then complete the new task information and save it as usual.

Now let's add one more task, using a few more of the options available in the Task window:

1. Click the New Task button to open a Task window, and type *Finish 5-year earnings projection for Sweet Forgiveness* in the Subject edit box. If necessary, maximize the window.

2. Click the arrow to the right of the Due Date edit box and in the drop-down calendar, select the date two weeks from today.

3. Click the arrow to the right of the Status edit box to show a list of options. You have already started this project, so select In Progress. (Outlook does not automatically enter the Start Date.)

    Changing a task's status

4. Then change the Priority setting to High.

5. This project is about half-finished, so click the up arrow next to the % Complete edit box twice to display 50%.

    Indicating progress

6. Now change the reminder date and time to the day before the project is due at 8:00 AM.

    Setting a reminder

7. Click an insertion point in the message box at the bottom of the dialog box and type *Be sure to compare data with Mona.*

8. Finally, click the Categories button, click the Clients check box, and click OK. The Task window now looks like this:

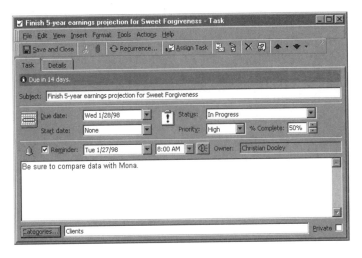

9. Click Save And Close to add the task to your to-do list.

Calendar vs. Tasks

In some ways, the Calendar and Tasks components of Outlook may seem alike. They both track the things we need to do and remind us about them. However, Tasks is much less time-conscious than Calendar. Once a reminder date and time have been reached, Tasks will continue to give daily reminders until the task has been designated as complete. Another difference is that Tasks can help you assign chores to other colleagues (see page 112).

Adding Recurring Tasks

Now suppose that on every other Friday, we have to perform a complete backup of the files we have created on our computer. To add a recurring task to our to-do list, we first create the task and then designate it as recurring. Follow these steps:

1. Click the New Task button on the toolbar and type *Perform complete data backup* in the Subject edit box.

2. Click the Recurrence button to display a dialog box similar to the one shown on page 82.

3. Check that Weekly is selected in the Recurrence Pattern section, change the Recur Every option to 2 weeks, and select the Friday check box (the check boxes for all other days should be deselected). The dialog box now looks like this:

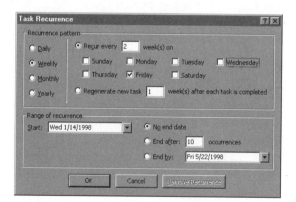

4. Click OK to close the Task Recurrence dialog box.

5. Back in the Task window, change the Reminder time to 1:00 PM and then click Save And Close. (In the to-do list, notice that Outlook displays a recurring icon in the Icon column for the data backup task.)

Editing Tasks

After creating a task, we may sometimes notice a typographical error that needs to be fixed or an item of information, such as a due date, that needs to be changed. We can make some

Setting reminder times

By default, reminder times for tasks are set for 8:00 AM. However, if you would prefer to be reminded at a different time of day, you can change the default setting. Choose Options from the Tools menu, and in the Tasks section of the Preferences Tab, type a new time in the Reminder Time edit box or click the arrow to the right of the box to select a time from the drop-down list. Then click OK.

changes directly in the to-do list, or we can reopen the Task window. Let's try both methods:

1. Click the earnings projection task and then select *Sweet Forgiveness*.

2. Replace the highlighted text with *Exotic Excursions* and then press Enter.

Suppose our supervisor has informed us that, because of database problems, the quarterly mutual fund performance report cannot be completed for another two weeks. Let's change its due date and priority level:

1. Double-click the performance report task to display its Task window.

2. Change the due date to two weeks after tomorrow and then reset the Priority to Normal.

3. Click Save And Close to update the task.

Designating Tasks as Complete

Adding tasks to the to-do list is only the first step if we want to manage our time effectively. We must also keep the status of our tasks up-to-date. Outlook's Tasks component provides several methods for showing that a task is complete.

Suppose we have picked up the dry cleaning and finished the Exotic Excursions 5-year earnings projection. Let's try a couple of different methods to show that these tasks are complete:

1. Click the check box in the Complete column of the dry cleaning task to designate the task as finished, as shown here:

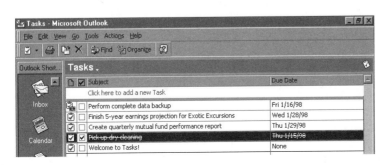

Copying tasks

Occasionally, you may want to create a new task that is similar to an existing one. You can speed up the process by copying the existing task. First, select the task you want to copy. Then hold down the Ctrl key and the left mouse button and drag the task anywhere in the to-do list. Release the mouse button and then the Ctrl key. (You can also use the Copy and Paste commands on the Edit menu to copy a task.) Then open the copy and make any changes that are necessary.

When you mark a task as complete, Outlook displays a check mark in the check box, changes the type color to gray, and crosses out the task text. It does not delete the task from the list. This way, you can view the list and double-check that you did in fact complete the task. (If Outlook simply erased the task, you might not remember whether you ever added it to the list in the first place.)

2. Next, double-click the earnings projection task to display its Task window and then choose Mark Complete from the Actions menu. Outlook closes the window and changes the display of the task in the to-do list to show that it is complete. (You can also change the Status edit box to Completed and then click Save And Close.)

The Details tab

When creating or editing a task, you can use the Details tab of the Task window to keep track of additional information about the task. Outlook automatically fills in the Date Completed field when you mark the task as complete. This information can be useful if you ever need to check the completion date of a project. In the Total Work field, you can enter the total number of hours you think the task will take to complete, and in the Actual Work field, you can enter the real number of hours it took. You use the remaining four fields to track mileage, billing information, and contacts or companies associated with the task. If you are working on a network that uses Exchange Server and you use Tasks to assign tasks to coworkers (we explain how on page 112), the Update List section lists all people whose task lists must be updated if a change is made to the task.

If we want, we can use the % Complete field to record the status of the task, or we can change it to 100% to show that the task is finished. We can update this field by displaying the Task window or by making changes directly in the % Complete field shown in Detailed List view. (We discuss this view on page 110.)

Deleting Completed Tasks

If we complete a task and no longer want to keep it on our to-do list, we can delete it. (Sometimes we may want to delete even an unfinished task.) Here's how to remove a task from the to-do list:

1. Click the dry cleaning task to select it.

2. Click the Delete button on the toolbar to remove the task from the list.

3. Delete Welcome To Tasks, if it is listed.

Like deleted items in other components, Outlook moves deleted tasks to the Deleted Items folder, where they remain until you erase a specific item from the folder or empty the folder completely.

Managing Tasks

Now that we know how to add, edit, and delete tasks, we need to cover some ways in which to categorize and organize them for maximum efficiency. As with other Outlook components, we can change the view of the to-do list. But before we take a look at the different views available for the Tasks component, we'll show you a quick way to reorganize the list. Follow these steps:

1. First, add a few more tasks to your to-do list using any of the methods we've discussed, so that you have a slightly longer list to work with. Your to-do list should then look something like this:

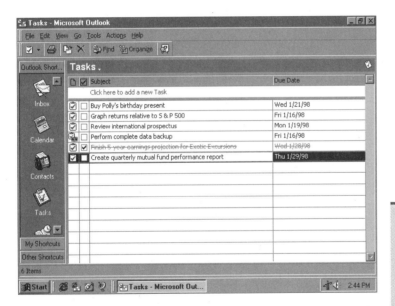

As you can see, the tasks are listed in the order in which you entered them, with the most recent entry at the top of the list. You might find it more useful, however, to list them in Due Date order.

2. Click the Due Date column header once to quickly reorganize the list chronologically by due date. Notice that Outlook has reorganized the list in descending order, symbolized by the down arrow in the column header.

Changing task text color schemes

By default, Outlook changes a completed task's text to gray and marks past due tasks in red. If you want to change the color scheme, choose Options from the Tools menu, and on the Preferences tab, click the Task Options button. In the dialog box that appears, click the arrow to the right of the Overdue Tasks or Completed Tasks edit boxes and select a new color from the drop-down list. Once you decide on a new color scheme, click OK twice to implement your changes.

3. To switch to ascending order, simply click the column header again. The list now looks like this:

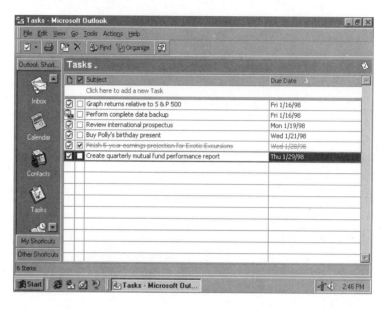

Let's take a look at other Tasks views. Follow these steps:

Switching views

1. Choose Current View from the View menu to display a submenu of ten view options.

2. Choose Detailed List to display the to-do list like this:

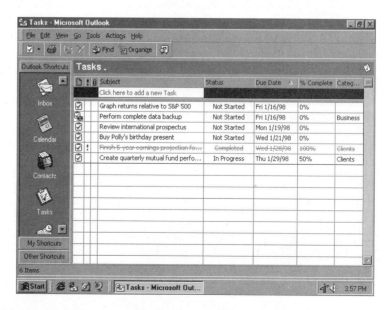

This view displays the Icon, Priority, Attachment, Subject, Status, Due Date, % Complete, and Categories fields. Notice that high priority tasks are flagged with an exclamation mark in the Priority column, and that switching views retains the Due Date sort order.

Before we look at the next view, we need to assign all the tasks to categories. Being able to categorize tasks is particularly useful if we work concurrently on different projects or if we like to keep track of personal as well as business tasks. Let's categorize the tasks now:

1. Select the first task, right-click it and choose Categories from the object menu to display the Categories dialog box shown earlier on page 12.

Assigning tasks to categories

2. Select the appropriate category from the list and click OK.

3. Repeat this procedure for the remaining tasks. When you finish, your to-do list looks something like this:

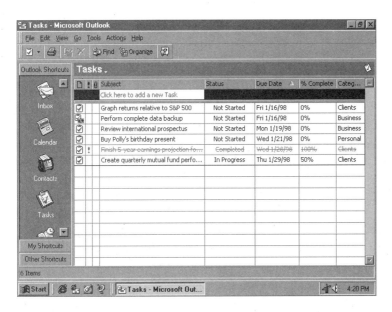

Now we're ready to use the By Category view to look at the to-do list. Follow these steps:

1. Choose Current View from the View menu and then choose By Category.

Other Tasks views

You may want to experiment with other Tasks views to help you organize your day. The Active Tasks view displays the same fields as the Detailed List view but displays only the tasks that have not been designated as complete. The Next Seven Days view focuses on the immediate tasks by displaying only the ones with due dates within the next week. With the Overdue Tasks view, you can focus on any tasks that have slipped through the cracks. The Assignment view displays the tasks you have given to others but that you track with an updated copy. (We discuss assigning tasks to others on this page.) The By Person Responsible view is similar to the Assignment view but groups the assigned tasks that you track by the people who now own them. (See the tip on the facing page for more information.) The Completed Tasks view lets you view what you have accomplished. Finally, the Task Timeline view displays a timeline with every task you have entered displayed in the appropriate section of the timeline. It shows the start date and due date of a task if that information was entered in the Task window, and when both dates are known, a gray bar indicates the interval between them. This view does not designate whether the task has been completed or not. (You can change the timeline view by clicking the Day, Week, or Month view buttons on the toolbar.)

2. Click the plus sign next to each category to display its contents like this:

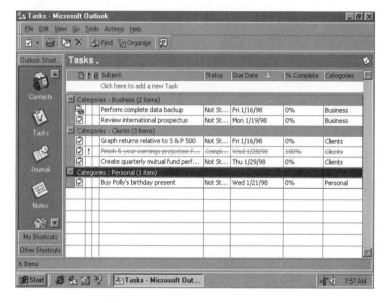

This view displays the same fields as the Detailed List view but it rearranges the tasks by category. (By default, the categories are grouped in ascending order.)

3. Experiment with some of the other task views (see the adjacent tip) and then return to the Simple List view.

Remember, you can customize any of these views or create completely new ones (see page 19).

Delegating Tasks

Before we wrap up this discussion of the Tasks component, we want to quickly discuss one more potentially useful feature. If you are using Outlook on a stand-alone computer, you can skip this section because it pertains only to those of you who are working with Outlook on a network that uses Exchange Server.

If we are managers or supervisors, part of our job is to delegate tasks to ensure that our company's business is carried out efficiently and economically. And we will probably need to keep tabs on the status of the tasks we delegate. Outlook's Tasks component can help us with these chores. Although we don't recommend eliminating face-to-face communication with your colleagues, we do suggest you experiment with this feature to see if it can help you manage projects better. Let's try it out now:

1. With the Tasks component active, choose New Task Request from the Actions menu to display this window, which is similar to the standard Task window:

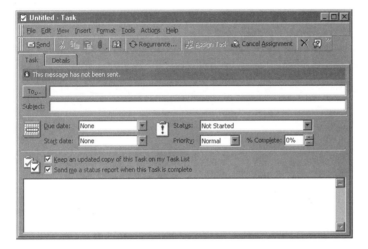

2. Type the e-mail address of the person to whom you want to delegate the task in the To edit box. (You can also click the To button to display the Select Task Recipient dialog box, which works like the Select Names dialog box shown on page 63.)

3. In the Subject edit box, type *Finish reviewing Sweet Forgiveness annual report.*

4. Click the arrow to the right of the Due Date edit box and assign a date two weeks from today.

5. Change the Status setting to In Progress and the Priority setting to High. Maximize the window and assign the task to the Clients category. The task now looks something like the one on the next page.

Owning tasks

Every time you create a new task, Outlook automatically designates you as the "owner" of the task unless you specify otherwise by assigning the task to someone else. If someone else accepts the task, he or she becomes the new owner even though you were the one who initially created the task. Also bear in mind that when you assign a task to several people, Outlook designates the first person listed in the To edit box as the owner of the task.

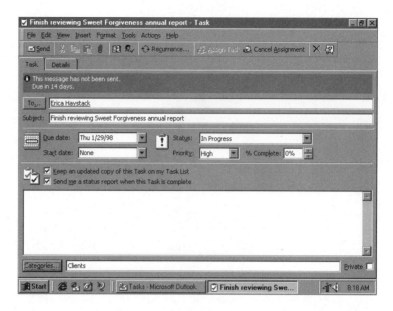

Notice the two check boxes above the message area of the window. If the Keep An Updated Copy check box is selected, Tasks tracks the progress of the task on a copy of it in your to-do list even if you assign the task to someone else and no longer "own" it. If the Send Me A Status Report check box is selected, the task recipient (the new "owner") can easily keep you posted on the task's status by clicking the Send Status Report button in the Task window to create a status report addressed to you (the original owner). If these check boxes are not selected, the task is removed from your to-do list.

6. To send the task, you would click the Send button. We won't actually send this task, so click the Close button and then click No when Outlook asks if you want to save your changes.

Assigning existing tasks

To assign an existing task to someone else, first open the task to display its window. Next, click the Assign Task button on the toolbar. The standard Task window is then converted into a Task Request window, and you can fill in the information as usual and click Send.

When we send a task assignment, the task shows up in our to-do list with a hand attached to the task's icon. If the recipient accepts or declines the task, notification shows up in our Inbox. Double-clicking the notification displays the Task window, which notes whether the task has been accepted. If the task has been declined, we can reassign the task. First, we must return the open task to our own to-do list by choosing Return To Task List from the Actions menu. Then the task can be reassigned following the procedure outlined in the tip on the facing page.

Dealing with a Task Request

If someone else delegates a task to us, we receive the task request in our Inbox just like a meeting request or an e-mail message. (The task is also added to our to-do list in bold type, indicating that we have yet to respond to it.) If we are working on a network that uses Exchange Server, we can open the message and respond to it using the Accept, Decline, or Assign Task buttons on the window's toolbar. When we accept or decline a task, Outlook displays a dialog box giving the option of either editing the response or sending the response immediately.

If we accept a task, it remains in our to-do list, and we become its owner, meaning we can make changes to its status, deadline, and so on. If we decline a task, the task is returned to the original owner, who can then reassign it. If we assign the task to someone else, either in the original request message or after accepting it, we follow the procedure for assigning an existing task described in the tip on the facing page.

That ends our discussion of Outlook's Tasks component. The more diligent we are about using and updating our to-do list, the more Outlook can help us keep our lives on track. Also remember that the usefulness of Outlook's Tasks component is augmented by the fact that a small version of the to-do list is displayed in the Calendar, which makes it easy to schedule time slots for specific tasks so that nothing slips through the cracks.

Reassigning tasks

Suppose you have assigned a task but now want to give it to a different colleague. If you selected the Keep An Updated Copy check box in the original Task Request window, you can open the updated copy of the task in your own to-do list. Next, click the Details tab and click the Create Unassigned Copy button. (See the tip on page 108 for more information about the Details tab.) Click OK in the message box that appears. You can then edit the copy of the original task request and send it to the new recipient(s). You will then need to notify the person to whom you originally designated the task of the change.

6
Checking Ahead and Looking Back

We fire up Outlook Today to see an overview of what's on our plate. Then we explore Outlook's Journal component, adding specific items to Journal's log and turning on Journal tracking for certain applications. Finally, we see how to archive old Outlook items.

Get an overview of the day's workload by using Outlook Today

Get regular updates on your Inbox status and your next appointment

Track items sent to and received by specified contacts

Use Journal to determine what documents you've worked on and when

So far, we have discussed the components of Outlook that we will probably use most frequently. As you'll see in a moment, we can check the contents of these components simultaneously by displaying Outlook Today in the workspace to get an overview of what we need to do. We can also use the Journal component to get an overview of what we've done. In this chapter, we'll take a brief look at Outlook's summary of what today has in store for us, and then we'll focus on how to look back at our past efforts.

Using Outlook Today

There's nothing complicated about Outlook Today. It simply gathers information about today's activities from Calendar, Tasks, and Inbox and summarizes them on one convenient screen. Now that we have entries in these three components, let's display Outlook Today in the workspace:

The Outlook Today icon

1. Click the Outlook Today icon on the Outlook bar to display an overview of the things you need to do today, as shown below. (We have added some appointments to Calendar for purposes of demonstration.)

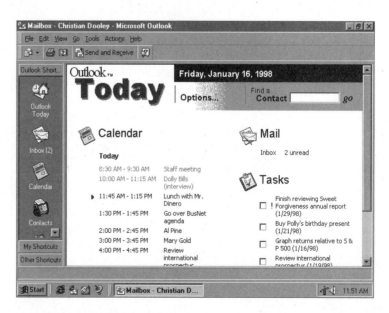

Notice that the next appointment is flagged with an arrow and that appointments earlier in the day appear in gray type.

2. Suppose you have finished the graphing task. Click its check box in the Tasks section. Outlook puts a check mark in the check box and strikes through the task text, like this:

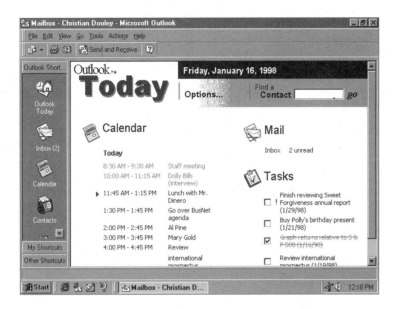

Marking tasks as complete from Outlook Today

3. Click the Tasks section heading to display the contents of Tasks in the workspace. Notice that the graphing task is marked as completed there, too. (You can click any section heading to jump directly to the corresponding component.)

Jumping to other components

4. Jump back to Outlook Today, type *Al Pine* in the Find A Contact edit box, and click Go. In the Check Names dialog box, double-click an Al Pine entry to jump to his Contact window, and then close the window without making any changes.

Finding contacts

Outlook Today provides an easy way of jumping among the various Outlook components we will use on a daily basis.

Making Outlook Today the Starting Component

Although Inbox is the Outlook component displayed in the workspace by default when we start the program, we will probably want to change this default once we have entered information in Calendar and Tasks and started receiving e-mail messages. Follow the steps on the next page.

Customizing Outlook Today ────────▶

1. Click Options at the top of Outlook Today. The workspace changes to display this list of the ways you can customize the Outlook Today screen:

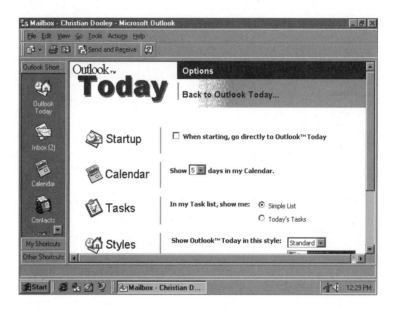

2. Click the When Starting, Go Directly To Outlook Today check box, and then click Back To Outlook Today.

Now whenever we start Outlook, the program will gather information about today's workload and display it for us.

Using Journal

As we work with Outlook, the Journal component can be active behind the scenes, logging the tasks we perform on the computer. (It can also log any work we do with the Microsoft Office applications.) We can record our own journal entries, and we can track our interactions with designated contacts. Then if we need to know how many hours we worked on a report in Word, or we want to check when we last talked with a client, we can easily track down this information. Journal can even act as a file manager and can help with archiving, which we discuss at the end of this chapter.

First, let's take a look at the Journal, and then we'll see what we can do with it. Follow these steps:

Other Outlook Today options

In the Outlook Today options window, you can designate how many days of your calendar you want displayed by clicking the arrow to the right of the Show edit box and choosing a number from the drop-down list. You can also tell Outlook whether to show a simple tasks list or just the tasks for the current date by clicking the appropriate option.

1. With Outlook open, click the Journal icon on the Outlook bar. ◄
   You see this message box:

The Journal icon

2. Click No to close the dialog box.

   Outlook will redisplay this dialog box the next time you click
   the Journal icon. After learning more about Journal, you can ◄
   click Yes to display the dialog box shown on page 125, where
   you can turn on Journal tracking for specific applications and
   contacts.

Turning on automatic
Journal tracking

   The current month's journal is displayed in the Outlook workspace, as shown below. (Check that By Type is the setting in
   the Current View submenu of the View menu.)

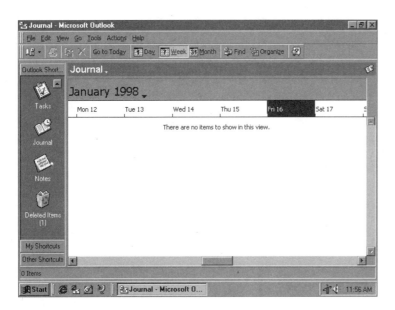

   Because you have not turned on Journal tracking, all you see
   is the timeline that helps you determine when you last worked
   with particular journal entries.

Creating Journal Entries

As we mentioned, we can create journal entries to track various Outlook items such as e-mail messages, task requests, or phone calls. We can also add journal entries for the documents we create. In this section, we'll add both types of journal entry.

Adding an Outlook Item

We can use a couple of different methods to add a journal entry for an Outlook item. First, let's create a journal entry for the interview with Dolly Bills:

The New Journal button

1. Click the New Journal button to display a blank Journal Entry window, as shown here:

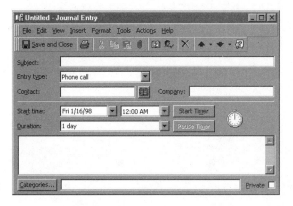

Other ways to add journal entries

If you have the Office shortcut bar installed (see the tip on page 8) and want to add a journal entry without opening Outlook, you can click the New Journal Entry button on the Office shortcut bar to quickly open the Journal Entry window. If Outlook is already open, you can choose New and then Journal Entry from the File menu. To use keyboard shortcuts, you can press Ctrl+N from within Journal or press Ctrl+Shift+J from any other Outlook component.

2. Type *Personnel* in the Subject edit box and then click the arrow to the right of the Entry Type edit box and select Meeting from the drop-down list.

3. Type *Dolly Bills* in the Contact edit box and then specify a week prior to today at 4:15 PM as the start time.

4. Next, change the Duration time to 2 hours.

5. In the message area, type *Initial interview went well. Bright, articulate, confident; annoying tendency to interrupt. If references check out, invite back for second interview with Mona.*

6. Assign the journal entry to the Business category and check the Private check box. Then click Save And Close. Outlook adds a *Meeting* entry type to Journal.

7. Click the plus sign next to the Meeting type and then scroll the horizontal scroll bar to display the entry, as shown here:

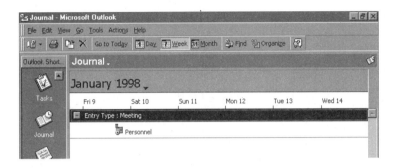

Notice the icon next to the entry name that designates this item as a journal entry. (Double-clicking a journal entry for a document doesn't open the document in its orginating application as you might expect. It opens the Journal Entry window for the document and displays information such as when the document was created, by whom, and the amount of time it was open.)

Now let's try an even easier method for adding journal entries by adding one for the Boston financial conference:

1. Switch to Calendar and activate the first day for the Boston financial conference by clicking its date in the Date Navigator.

2. Point to the conference entry at the top of the day's time slots and drag it to the Journal icon. Outlook displays a partially filled in Journal Entry window, as shown here:

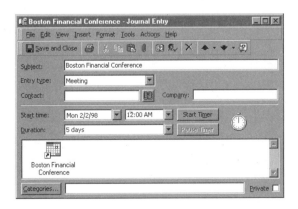

Recording phone calls with Journal

To have Journal record only phone calls for a particular contact, you cannot use the method described in the tip on the next page. Instead you must first place the call as usual (see the tip on page 54 for more information about placing phone calls). Then, in the New Call dialog box, click the Create New Journal Entry check box to record the call. Click the Start Call button to place the call. When you hang up, Journal adds an entry for the call. However, if you have specified that Journal automatically record any (or all) other activities for a contact, either on the Journal tab of the Contact window (see the tip on page 39) or in the Journal Options dialog box (see the tip on the next page), Journal will also record phone calls placed through Outlook to that contact even though a phone call option is not available for you to select.

3. Click an insertion point to the right of the appointment's icon in the message area, type *Great conference; very informative; definitely will attend next year*, and click Save And Close.

4. Switch back to Journal to view your new entry as shown below. (If it's not visible, click the arrow to the right of the month in the timeline to display a date navigator and click the appropriate date to move to that section in the timeline.)

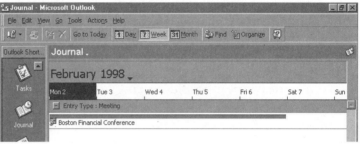

Changing Journal tracking defaults

By default, Journal tracking records three types of activities: creating or opening any Office files; sending and receiving any e-mail messages or task requests to and from any specified contacts; and placing any phone call through Outlook. If you want to change these defaults, you can do so by choosing Options from the Tools menu, displaying the Preferences tab, and then clicking the Journal Options button. You can then select what type of Outlook items you want Journal to record for designated contacts. (This is a choice affecting all designated contacts. You cannot automatically record only e-mail messages for Mona Terry while automatically recording both e-mail messages and task requests for Ann Damand.) In the Also Record Files From list at the bottom of the dialog box, you can specify which Office documents Journal should track. You can also change the default double-click behavior (see page 127) and set autoarchiving options (see page 130).

Adding a Contact Activity

In the tip on page 39 in Chapter 2, we briefly discussed how to track activities such as placing phone calls and sending e-mail messages to contacts in your Contacts list. Now let's take a more in-depth look at how this works. Follow these steps:

1. Click the Contacts icon, double-click the header for your own address card, and in the Contact window, click the Journal tab to display these options:

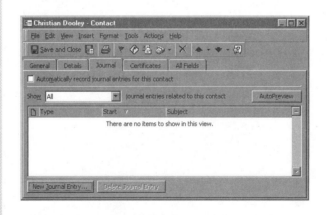

2. Click the Automatically Record Journal Entries check box and click Save And Close.

3. Choose Options from the Tools menu, and on the Preferences tab, click the Journal Options button to display this dialog box:

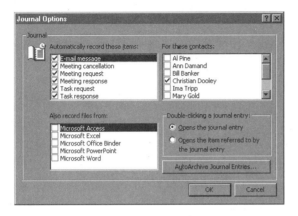

4. Check that E-mail Message is selected in the Automatically Record These Items section, and click OK twice.

5. With your address card still selected in the Contacts window, click the New Message To Contact button on the toolbar to display a Message window, type yourself a message, and then click Send.

The New Message To Contact button

6. Switch to Inbox and if necessary, click the Send And Receive button on the toolbar to send and receive any new messages.

7. Switch back to Contacts, double-click your address card in the workspace, and click the Journal tab of the Contact window, where Outlook has recorded your e-mail message:

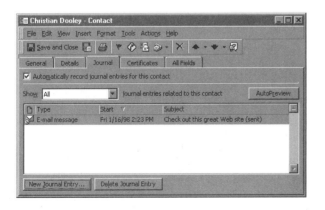

Displaying contacts from journal entries

If a person listed in your contacts list is associated with a particular journal entry, you can display his or her Contact window from Journal. Double-click the journal entry to open its window and then double-click the underlined name in the Contact edit box. (If the name is not underlined, that person has not been added to your contacts list.)

You can create a new journal entry by clicking the New Journal Entry button at the bottom of the tab or you can erase an entry by selecting it in the list and then clicking the Delete Journal Entry button.

8. Close the Contact window.

Adding a Document

As we mentioned, we can set up Outlook to automatically track files created by Office applications. We can also manually add journal entries for documents created in other programs. In the following steps, we use My Computer to show you how:

The My Computer icon

1. Click the Other Shortcuts button to display its group of icons on the Outlook bar. Then click the My Computer icon to display its contents in the workspace, as shown here:

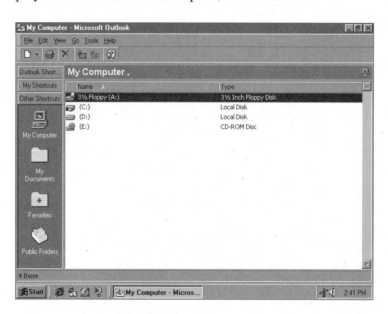

2. Navigate to a file for which you want to add a journal entry and then click it once to select it.

3. Click the Outlook Shortcuts button on the Outlook bar and drag the file in My Computer to the Journal icon. When you release the mouse button, Outlook displays a Journal Entry window with most of the information filled in.

4. Add any other information you want for this entry and then click Save And Close.

5. Click the Journal icon to redisplay its contents.

Using Journal as a File Manager

Although Journal's main function is to record journal entries for documents and Outlook items, we can also use it to open files that have recorded entries. And we can use Journal to display contact information for any contacts associated with a particular file (see the tip on page 125). Let's try opening a file from Journal now:

1. Display the journal entry you just created for the document by clicking the Document entry type's plus sign and if necessary, scrolling the workspace.

Opening documents
from Journal

2. Right-click the entry and choose Open Item Referred To from the object menu. Outlook instantly opens the item in its originating application.

3. Close the application to return to Outlook.

   If we keep Outlook open all the time and frequently open documents from Journal, we can change Outlook's default behavior so that by double-clicking the journal entry, we open the entry's document instead of opening the journal entry. Follow these steps to make this change:

1. Choose Options from the Tools menu and click Journal Options on the Preferences tab.

2. In the Double-Clicking A Journal Entry section, select the Opens The Item option, and click OK twice.

3. Now double-click the document you opened earlier to test the change. Then close the application.

4. To display the journal entry instead, right-click the item and then choose Open Journal Entry from the object menu.

5. Close the Journal Entry window.

Starting new documents from Journal

If you have the Office shortcut bar installed (see the tip on page 8), you can easily open a new Office document. However, you can open a new document for any program from within Outlook. First, open the program and load a new, blank document. Choose Save As from the program's File menu and save the file as *New* with the program's default extension. You can then display the storage location of the file in Outlook and double-click the *New* document to both launch the program and open a new, blank document. To safeguard the New document, choose Save As immediately from the File menu, assign a file name, and specify the storage location.

Customizing Journal

To wrap up our discussion of the Journal component of Outlook, let's take a look at some of its views so that you can determine which one best suits your needs. First, let's take a closer look at the default By Type timeline view:

Tracking Office documents

1. If Office is installed on your computer, turn on Journal tracking for its applications by choosing Options from the Tools menu, clicking Journal Options, selecting the appropriate check boxes in the Also Record Files From section and clicking OK twice.

2. Create two new documents in each of the tracked applications, or open and close existing documents.

3. Back in Journal, display the entries for one of the applications. We chose the Microsoft Word entry type, as shown below:

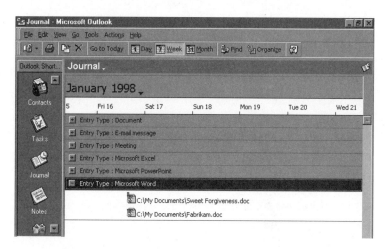

If we work on several documents in a particular application on consecutive days, we may have difficulty deciphering this timeline view. Because the entire document path must be visible, Outlook stacks journal entries that could otherwise overlap. As a result, the list of journal entries may not seem to be in chronological order and particular items can get hard to find. Let's change the timeline view to avoid this problem:

Changing the Journal view

1. Click the Month button on the toolbar to display a timeline that looks something like the one shown on the facing page.

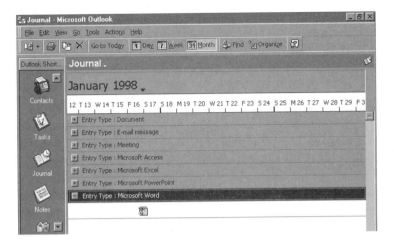

The labels have disappeared altogether, and it is now even more difficult to tell when a document was last worked on.

2. Point to any journal entry. Outlook displays a label for the entry in a pop-up box.

                ← Displaying more information

3. Click the Day button to display yet another timeline view as shown here:

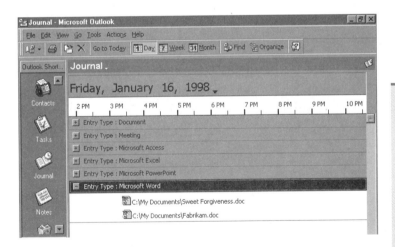

As you can see, this view gives you an hourly picture of which documents you worked on and when. (You can also open an item's Journal Entry window to see how long you worked on that item.)

Assigning journal entries to categories

You can assign a journal entry to a category by clicking the Category button in its Journal Entry window. But if several entries belong in the same category, there is a faster way. First, hold down the Ctrl key and select all the journal entries you want to assign to a particular category. Then, right-click the selected items and choose Categories from the object menu. In the Categories dialog box, click the appropriate category and then click OK.

4. Click the Week button to return to the default view.

Before we end this section, let's look at one of Journal's table views, which we often find is the clearest way to organize journal entries. Try this:

1. Choose Current View and then Entry List from the View menu. The Journal window now looks like this:

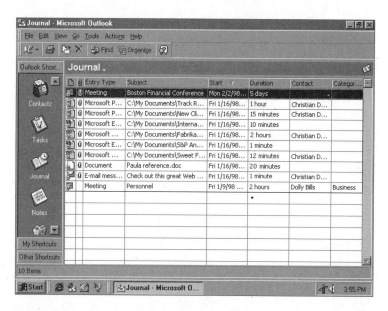

Other Journal views

Outlook offers four other pre-defined Journal views: By Contact, By Category, Last Seven Days, and Phone Calls. The By Contact and By Category views are timeline views with grouping boxes for either contact names or categories. The Last Seven Days view is a table view that displays only entries up to seven days old. The Phone Calls view is another table view that displays only phone calls made through Outlook. Remember, you can modify these views to suit your tastes, and you can create completely new ones.

In this view we see Icon, Attachment, Entry Type, Subject, Start, Duration, Contact, and Categories columns. As with the other Outlook views, this view can be customized to show only the information we need. (See page 19 for more information.) We'll leave you to experiment with customization on your own. (See the adjacent tip for more information about other Journal views.)

Archiving Outlook Files

As promised, we are going to end this chapter with a discussion of archiving Outlook files. The more we use Outlook, the more its files will grow. (The size of the files can increase pretty quickly if we have certain options selected; see the tip on the facing page.) If we archive old Outlook files, we can keep the current files at a reasonable size. We can always retrieve the archived files if we need to look up old information (see the tip on the next page). We can have Outlook automatically archive our files at specified intervals, or we can do the archiving manually. Let's look at both methods:

1. Choose Folder List from the View menu to display the folders for each Outlook component.

2. Right-click the Calendar folder, and choose Properties from the object menu. Then click the AutoArchive tab of the Calendar Properties dialog box to display these options:

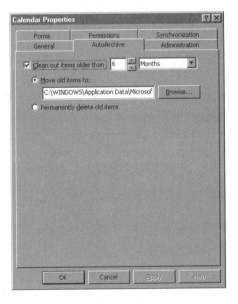

Old Calendar items will be moved to a file called *archive.pst* in a subfolder of the Windows folder. If you want to save the archived files in another location, you can either enter the path in the Move Old Items To edit box or use the Browse button. Notice that you can select the Permanently Delete Old Items option to delete the items instead of archiving them.

3. Check that the Clean Out Items Older Than check box is selected and then set the time to 3 months (or select the time interval you think is most appropriate for your work).

4. Click OK to apply the new setting.

Maintaining a small Outlook file

Here are some preventative measures you can take to maintain a small Outlook file, some of which have already been mentioned in this book:

- Try to empty the Deleted Items folder on a regular basis. (You can tell Outlook to automatically empty this folder every time you exit Outlook by choosing Options from the Tools menu, clicking the Other tab, and clicking the Empty The Deleted Items Folder Upon Exiting check box.)

- Turn off the option to save copies of sent and forwarded messages (see the tip on page 69).

- Only record necessary journal entries. If you find you don't use the feature at all, don't record any journal entries.

- Archive your files frequently so that Outlook can get rid of old files.

- Compact your personal folder files by choosing Services from the Tools menu. Select Microsoft Exchange Server on the Services tab and click the Properties button. Click the Advanced tab and then click the Offline Folder File Settings button. Finally, click the Compact Now button. When Outlook is finished compacting the files, click OK three times to close all the dialog boxes.

5. Repeat this procedure for all the other Outlook folders except Contacts, which contains only active items. (Outlook may not automatically select the Clean Out Items check box for some folders, so you may need to select it first.)

Now we need to verify that the AutoArchive feature is activated. Follow these steps:

Setting AutoArchive options

1. Choose Options from the Tools menu, click the Other tab, and click the AutoArchive button to display these options:

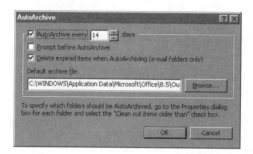

Here, you can specify how often you want the archiving procedure to occur, whether you want to be prompted or not, and whether expired e-mail messages should be sent to the Deleted Items folder. If you select the Prompt Before Auto-Archive check box, Outlook displays a message box when it is ready to begin archiving. If you click No to delay archiving,

Restoring an archived file

You can use one of two methods to restore archived Outlook files. If you know you need the files only temporarily, open them as separate Personal Folders. To use this method, choose Open from the File menu and then choose Personal Folders File (.pst). Navigate to the archive file you want to open and click OK in the Open Personal Folders dialog box. Outlook then adds a Personal Folders folder to Outlook's folder list. You simply open and close the folders as usual to get to the information you need. When you have finished using the archived files, right-click the appropriate Personal Folders file and choose Close "Personal Folders" from the object menu. The second method requires you to import the archived file into your existing Personal Folders file. (If necessary, choose New and then Personal Folders File (.pst) from the File menu. Navigate to the Outlook folder in the Create Personal Folders dialog box and click Create. Then click OK to accept the default in the Create Microsoft Personal Folders dialog box.) Choose Import And Export from the File menu, select Import From Another Program Or File, and click Next. Select Personal Folder File (.pst) as the file type and click Next. Select the file you want to import by using the Browse button, and select the duplicates option you want in the Options section. Then click Next. Select the folder and any subfolders you want to import, check that Personal Folders is selected in the Import Items Into The Same Folder In box, and click Finish. Outlook imports the files in the designated locations, and they are then ready for you to use.

Outlook reminds you about archiving every time you open the program, until you complete the process.

2. If you want, change any settings to meet your particular needs and then click OK twice.

Here are the steps for archiving files manually:

1. Choose Archive from the File menu to display the dialog box shown here:

Archiving files manually

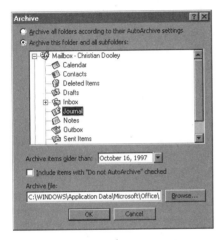

You can use the two options at the top of the dialog box to either archive according to the settings specified in each component's Properties dialog box or to select a specific folder (or all of them if you select your Mailbox folder) and archive all items older than a certain date. To specify the date, click the arrow to the right of the Archive Items Older Than edit box and select a date in the date navigator.

2. We aren't actually going to archive right now, so click Cancel to close the dialog box.

As you have seen, by faithfully using Outlook's Journal, as well as the program's archiving features, we can keep better track of our time and maintain additional information about the items we work on.

Accessing the Internet via Outlook

7

In this chapter, we plunge into the World Wide Web and learn how to find the information we need. Then we explore newsgroups and discuss online etiquette. Finally, we fire up NetMeeting and try our hands at chatting, collaborating, and videoconferencing.

Subscribe to the newsgroups you want to participate in

Post articles and follow-ups using the Compose Message and Reply To Group buttons

Display articles in the preview pane or double-click the header to see the article in its own window

Download all the articles in a newsgroup to catch up on the current discussions

Set up a call and then communicate in a variety of ways

Set up a videoconference if you have sound and video equipment

In Chapter 3, we discussed how to communicate with the outside world using Internet e-mail. In this chapter, we'll briefly cover other ways to take advantage of the Internet while working with Outlook. First, we discuss Internet Explorer and how to browse the part of the Internet known as the *World Wide Web*. Then we see how we can share our ideas and insights by participating in *newsgroups*, which we access using the news reader that comes with Outlook Express. Finally, we take a look at *NetMeeting*, which we can use to communicate with others in various ways, including holding audio- and videoconferences.

What you need →

To take advantage of the Internet services available with Outlook, we need the following:

- **TCP/IP.** This protocol for transferring information over the Internet must be installed on our computer.

- **Modem.** We install a modem on our computer by using the Modems icon in Control Panel, or we must be able to access a network modem.

- **Internet access.** We must have an account with an Internet service provider (ISP), or our company or organization must provide Internet access.

- **Dial-Up Networking.** If Internet access is via an ISP and through a modem connected to our computer, we must have Dial-Up Networking installed, and we must set up a Dial-Up Networking connection so that our computer can talk to the ISP's computer over phone lines.

- **Internet proxy server.** If Internet access is via our network, we need to give Windows information about the proxy server (available from the network administrator).

The technical details of installing these necessary tools is beyond the scope of this book, and you should enlist the help of your network administrator or your ISP in getting everything set up just right. Once you have a working Internet connection established, join us for the next section, where we use Internet Explorer to take a quick look at the Web.

Browsing with Internet Explorer

To surf the Internet or a company *intranet* (see the tip below), we can use Microsoft's Web browser program, Internet Explorer, which comes with Outlook 98. We can't do more than briefly introduce Internet Explorer here, but what we do cover should give enough information for you to be able to explore further on your own. (If you want more detailed information about Internet Explorer, you may want to take a look at *Quick Course in Internet Explorer 4.0*, another book in the Quick Course series.)

Let's fire up Internet Explorer and check it out:

1. First, to give yourself more space on the screen to explore the Web, right-click a blank area of the Windows taskbar and then choose Properties from the object menu. Next, click the AutoHide check box found on the Taskbar Options tab and click OK. (When you want to display the taskbar, simply point to the bottom of the screen and the taskbar will appear for as long as you point to it.)

   Hiding the taskbar

2. Start Outlook and choose Web Browser from the Go menu.

   Accessing Internet Explorer via Outlook

3. If Windows asks you to connect to your ISP, click Connect. After some initial activity, Internet Explorer displays the home page of Microsoft's Web site, which is called *Internet Start*. (Don't worry if you see a different starting page.)

   The Microsoft Web site

4. Check that the first part of the entry in the Address box across the top of the window (under the toolbar) is

   http://home.microsoft.com/

   (This entry is called a *universal resource locator*, or *URL*; see the tip on the next page for more information.) If your entry is different from this, then click the current entry to select it. Next, type *http://home.microsoft.com/*, and press Enter. Your screen now looks something like the one shown on the following page.

Intranets

Using Internet technology, many companies are setting up Internet servers and creating Web look-alikes called *intranets*, which are accessible only from the company's computers. The intranet enables people to easily and cheaply access company information, exchange ideas, and collaborate on projects. A system of security "firewalls" ensures that the intranet information is available only to the people in the company who are authorized to access it.

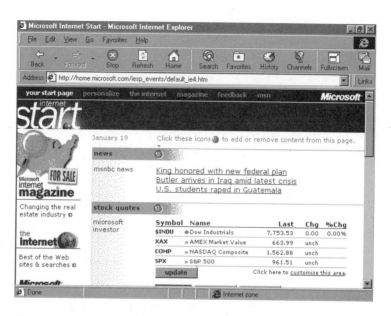

The anatomy of a URL

To better understand URLs, we can break down an address, such as *http://home.microsoft.com*, into its component parts. The *http* component of a URL stands for *HyperText Transfer Protocol*, which is the name for the set of rules used on the Web. Next comes the *domain name*, which is the name of the computer (or *server*) on which the Web resource is stored. These names usually consist of two or more parts joined together by periods. Domain names of servers in the US usually end in *com* for a company, *edu* for an educational institution, *gov* for a government agency, *mil* for a military agency, *net* for network administration support, and *org* for another type of organization. The domain name may be followed by a slash and a series of directory and file names that pinpoint the exact location of the information displayed in the viewing area.

Your viewing area probably looks different from ours because Microsoft changes this Web site at least once a day.

Confused by all the terms we've used so far? We assume you know what the Internet and the Web are, but here's a quick run down of three other terms:

- **Web site.** An informational resource published by a government agency, company, organization, or individual on the Web. Sites consist of text, graphics, and multimedia components such as audio and video files, all coded in such a way that they can be viewed by Web browsers.

- **URL.** The address of a Web site (see the adjacent tip).

- **Home page.** The starting point of a Web site. For ease of viewing, the information stored at a Web site is divided into chunks called *pages*. You can move from one page to another within a Web site—and even from site to site—by clicking *hyperlinks*, which are coded addresses of related information that are attached to text or other elements on a page.

Moving Around

Now let's see these elements in action. Web sites can change dramatically over time, and frequently sites that are here today are gone tomorrow. For purposes of demonstration, we'll take you to the Quick Course Web site—a site that we know hasn't changed—and show you around it. Follow these steps:

1. Click the URL in the Address box to select it.

2. Now type *www*, then a period, then *quickcourse.com*, and press Enter. Because the URL begins with *www*, Internet Explorer automatically adds *http://* in front of it. (You may have to type *http://* for URLs that don't begin with *www*.) After a flurry of activity, Internet Explorer displays this Quick Course home page:

The Quick Course Web site

As you'll see, reading the information at a Web site is not like reading a book. Follow these steps to get a feel for how Web information is organized and how to move around:

1. Move the pointer over the row of graphics below the title, noticing that the pointer changes to a hand to indicate that the graphics are hyperlinks (don't click anything yet).

Graphic hyperlinks

2. Scroll through the home page using the scroll bar, and move the pointer over the underlined words without clicking. Notice that the pointer changes to a hand when positioned over these text hyperlinks.

Text hyperlinks

Jumping to a different page

3. Scroll to the top of the home page, point to the *Catalog* graphic hyperlink, and with the pointer shaped like a hand, click the left mouse button. Your screen now looks like this:

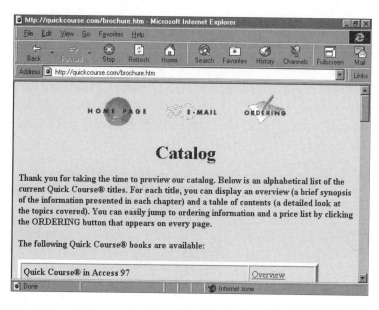

4. Scroll the title list until you see *Quick Course in Office 97*, and click the *Overview* text hyperlink to jump to a new page.

Suppose we want to go back to the title list to check out a different book. Internet Explorer provides Back and Forward buttons on its toolbar that we can use to move through the pages we have already displayed, no matter which Web site those pages belong to. Try this:

The Back button

1. Click the Back button on the toolbar to redisplay the catalog page, and then click the button once again to redisplay the home page.

The Forward button

2. Click the Forward button to redisplay the catalog page, and notice that the *Overview* hyperlink for the *Quick Course in Office 97* title has changed color to remind you that you have already viewed the information on that page.

3. Scroll to *Quick Course in Internet Explorer 4*, and click its *Overview* hyperlink.

Some Web pages provide hyperlinks we can use to move directly from one part of the site to another. Try this:

1. Scroll to the bottom of the Internet Explorer Overview page and click the Home Page graphic to move directly back to the Quick Course home page, the first page of this Web site. (Most well-designed sites include a hyperlink back to the home page from all the other pages in the site. This feature is most useful if you have been surfing for some time and the Back and Forward button lists have become cumbersome.)

2. Scroll the home page, click the *frequently asked questions* hyperlink, and then click the first question, *What is a Quick Course® book?* This is what you see:

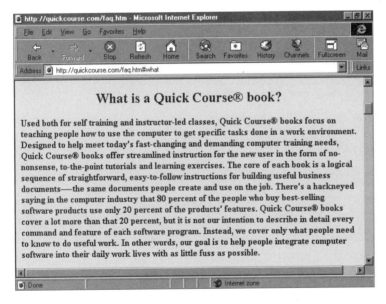

3. Click the Back button and then scroll the frequently asked questions page. Notice that it contains the list of questions at the top, followed by the answers. The hyperlinks we used previously all jumped to a linked file (a different page) that is stored at the same Web site, whereas each question hyperlink jumps to a linked place within the same file (the same page).

Frequently asked questions (FAQs)

So many Web sites include a frequently asked questions page that these pages have become known as *FAQs*. Clicking a hyperlink labeled *FAQ* usually takes you to a list of common questions and answers, so this is a good place to start when you are looking for information.

The Home button

4. Test the hyperlinks at the Quick Course Web site until you can move around with ease. Then click the Home button on the toolbar to display the Internet Explorer starting page.

5. If you have been collecting the addresses of Web sites you want to check out, enter one of them in the Address box and explore another Web site now. (Remember, if you get lost, click the Home button to come back to familiar territory.)

Searching for Information

Microsoft's Internet Start page provides ways of finding information on the Web, as well as information about Microsoft products, and you will want to explore its many features on your own. Here, we want to show you another way of tracking down the information you need. To do research on the Web, **Web databases** we can search a Web database—a collection of information about Web sites and their content. Several databases are available, but we'll take a look at only Yahoo here. Because the techniques for searching are pretty similar for all the databases, you'll be able to check out the others on your own later. For now, follow these steps:

The Yahoo Web site

1. Click the Address box, type *www.yahoo.com*, and press Enter to jump to Yahoo's home page, as shown here:

The History and Search buttons

If you want to return to a Web site you visited within the last week, you can click the History button to display a list of previously visited sites organized by day and week. Find the site you want to return to and click it. If you want to search for information but don't know the Web addresses of the available databases, you can click the Search button to access the Search panel, where you can select a database from the Select Provider drop-down list to display its home page.

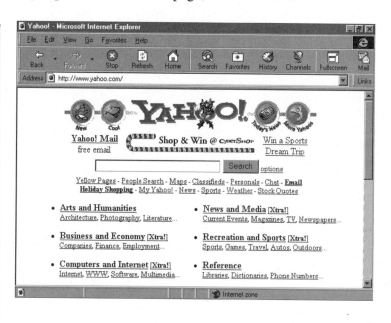

2. Ignore the Search box at the top of the page for now and scroll through the available categories, noting their subcategories for future searches.

3. Under *Regional*, click *U.S. States*. Then scroll the page and click your state.

Searching for city information

4. On the state page, click *Cities*. Then click your city (or the closest one). Yahoo displays information about the area in which you live.

5. Click the arrow to the right of the Back button and select *Ya-hoo!* from the drop-down list to return to the Yahoo home page.

6. Click *Weather* below the Search box, click *United States*, click your state, and then click your city to see the weather for your area.

Searching for weather information

7. Again, click the arrow to the right of the Back button and se-lect *Yahoo!* from the drop-down list.

Suppose we want to search for information about digital cam-eras and we haven't a clue which category to look in. We can use a keyword search instead of a category search to track down the information. Try this:

1. At the top of the Yahoo home page, click an insertion point in the Search box, type *digital+cameras*, and click the Search button. Then click Yes when Internet Explorer displays a Se-curity Alert dialog box. Yahoo searches through its database for the keywords you entered and displays the results.

2. Scroll through Yahoo's findings (called *hits*), clicking the hyper-links of any that look promising.

When it's time to end an Internet session, the procedure we use depends on our Internet service provider. In the following steps, substitute the procedure appropriate for your setup:

1. Click the Close button at the right end of the Internet Explorer title bar to quit the program.

2. In the Disconnect dialog box, click Yes.

Constructing keyword searches

To get meaningful results from a Web search, you have to con-struct your search criteria very carefully to narrow down the re-sults as much as possible. For ex-ample, if you want information on climbing gyms in Boise, you might try typing *Boise climbing gyms* as your search criteria. How-ever, the results of the search would give you Web sites containing the words *Boise* or *climbing* or *gyms*—possibly more than 50,000 sites! To search on the exact string of the words *Boise climbing gyms*, enclose the text in double quota-tion marks (" "). If you want to find sites that contain both the phrase *climbing gyms* and the word *Boise*, but not necessarily together, type *+Boise+"climbing gyms"*. The plus sign tells the search en-gine that the results must contain the word(s) following the plus sign. To exclude a word, type a minus sign.

Participating in Newsgroups

The term *newsgroups* refers to a vast collection of public discussion groups that are accessible via the Internet. Newsgroups are the closest thing the Internet has to a community bulletin board, where we can check out the latest messages about a mind-boggling number of subjects. We can passively read these messages or actively participate in a discussion by contributing our own messages.

In this section, we show you how to use the news reader that comes with Outlook Express, a component of Internet Explorer, to join the online discussions available through Usenet, the largest newsgroup system. Internet service providers can use one of their servers to carry all or some of the Usenet newsgroups, and many ISPs carry other newsgroups as well, including some that cater to local interests. However, some ISPs don't carry newsgroups at all. As long as your ISP has a news server, you can tap into this huge reservoir of information and social interaction without any additional software. Follow these steps to see what to do:

1. With Outlook open on your screen, choose News from the Go menu to start the news reader of Outlook Express. Your screen looks like this:

Usenet categories

Usenet newsgroups are divided into general categories like these:

biz	Business (commercial)
comp	Computer-related
K12	Teaching and students
misc	Miscellaneous topics
news	Usenet information
rec	Recreation and leisure activities
sci	Science (except for computer science, which is in comp)
soc	Social issues and all kinds of socializing
talk	Topic-based, often heated discussions

You might also have access to the catch-all *alt* (for *alternative*) category of Usenet newsgroups, which includes everything that doesn't fit into the other categories, including lifestyle groups and pornography posing as art (or simply posing!).

2. Click Read News in the right pane. If newsgroup access is already set up on your computer, you see a dialog box like the one shown here:

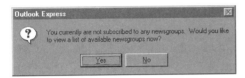

If newsgroup access is not yet set up on your computer, the Internet Connection Wizard starts itself so that you can tell Outlook Express the domain name of the server that handles newsgroups and so that you can enter some pertinent information about yourself. You can then enter the requested information (see the adjacent tip) and click the Next button to move from one dialog box to the next dialog box. Then in the wizard's last dialog box, click Finish to save your news settings. You will then see the dialog box like the one that's shown above.

3. Click Yes. If you see a dialog box asking whether you want to connect to your news server, click Yes again and, if necessary, click the Connect button. Outlook Express then downloads the newsgroup list from your server. Once the list is downloaded and saved in a file on your hard drive, you see a Newsgroups dialog box like the one shown here:

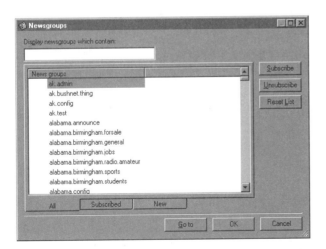

Setting up the news reader

To set up the Outlook Express news reader, you will need to enter the following:

- Your first and last name (for example, *Jill Doe*).

- Your full Internet e-mail address (for example, *jdoe@halcyon.biz*).

- The name of your news (NNTP) server (for example, *news.halcyon.biz*). If your ISP requires you to log on to the news server, click the check box at the bottom of this dialog box.

- A friendly name that Outlook Express will use for your news settings (for example, *Jill Doe's News Settings*).

- Your Internet connection type (if you use a modem to connect to your ISP, select Connect Using My Phone Line; otherwise, select Connect Using My Local Area Network).

- Information about your dial-up connection.

In the next section, we'll find out what newsgroups are available and show you how to move around.

Browsing Newsgroups

Learning about Usenet ──────────►

For efficiency, every Usenet user should read a few specific newsgroups before setting off on broader exploration. The *news* newsgroups category offers a wealth of information about how to get started with newsgroups, as well as some interesting historical Usenet background.

Let's take a look at the *news.announce.newusers* group. (If this newsgroup is not available, use *news.answers* instead.) Try this:

1. Type *news* in the Display Newsgroups Which Contain edit box. Now the list box shows only the newsgroups that contain the word *news* in their names.

2. Scroll the list box until you see *news.announce.newusers,* select it, and click the Go To button. Outlook Express retrieves about 300 of the group's messages, called *articles,* from your news server and displays their headers in the Outlook Express window, like this:

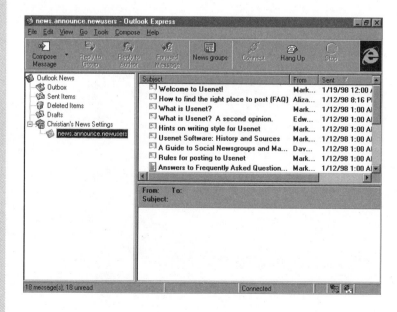

More about the *news* newsgroups

We strongly recommend that you read the articles in the *news.announce.newusers* and *news.answers* groups before you post any articles of your own, and we explain in the tip on the facing page how to save these articles on your hard disk as files so that you can read them offline. These articles were written by newsgroup veterans and offer sound advice on how to participate in newsgroups. (They reinforce the information we provide in this chapter.) We don't recommend that you read the articles in the *news.newusers.questions* newsgroup. Often these articles are posted by people who haven't bothered to read either the *news.announce.newusers* or *news.answers* articles, and who can't wait to post something—*anything*—to a newsgroup. The only use we have found for the articles in this newsgroup is that they provide examples of what *not* to do in other newsgroups if you want to avoid the scorn of the Usenet community.

In the top right pane is the subject, the sender's name, the date and time the article was posted, and (out of view) the size of the message. When we have not yet read an article, its header is displayed in bold type. By the way, the list of articles on your screen will be different from ours because new newsgroup articles are posted constantly. ISPs set expiration policies that range from one day to a few weeks for each newsgroup, and articles are automatically removed according to those expiration policies. Because the *news.announce.newusers* newsgroup is an important reservoir of basic information about Usenet, its articles are regularly reposted to the newsgroup to keep them available. Even so, your list won't be exactly the same as ours. (The articles you'll see in the other newsgroups we'll visit will also vary from those on our screens.)

3. Scroll the headers in the top pane, noticing that some articles answer frequently asked questions (FAQs) and some provide more general information.

4. In the top pane, click an article header, such as *Answers to Frequently Asked Questions about Usenet*. Outlook Express displays the article in the preview pane with a header bar, much like an e-mail message header, across the top.

5. Double-click the header in the top pane to display the article in its own window, and scroll the article to see its information, like this:

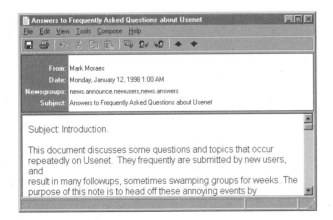

6. Close the window.

← Expiring articles

← Previewing articles

Saving articles to read offline

If you find an article you want to read that is fairly long, you probably don't want to spend time reading it online. Instead, you can save the article as a file so that you can read it later. With the article displayed in the preview pane of the Outlook Express window, choose Save As from the File menu. Type a filename for the article, change the Save As Type setting to Text Files, move to the desired storage folder, and click Save to save the file. Now you can read the article at your leisure by opening it in a word-processing program. As an alternative to saving an article, you can simply print it. To do so, choose Print from the File menu.

Subscribing to Newsgroups

When we find a newsgroup we want to participate in, or at least check regularly for new articles, we can *subscribe* to it. Don't worry: subscribing doesn't mean we have to fork over any money. We subscribe to a newsgroup to tell Outlook Express that we have more than a passing interest in it. We can then display only the newsgroups to which we have subscribed.

As a demonstration of how to subscribe to a newsgroup, let's look for investment information that might be useful to the consultants at Ferguson and Bardell, our fictional money management company. First, we need to find a newsgroup frequented by investors:

The News Groups button

1. Start by clicking the News Groups button on the toolbar to open the Newsgroups dialog box shown on page 145, and then type *invest* (for *investments*).

2. Click the *misc.invest.mutual-funds* newsgroup to select it and then click the Subscribe button on the right. Outlook Express displays an icon to the left of the group name.

3. Select *misc.invest.stocks* and click the Subscribe button.

4. Next, subscribe to *misc.invest.options*.

5. Click the Subscribed tab in the Newsgroups dialog box to display only the subscribed newsgroups, like this:

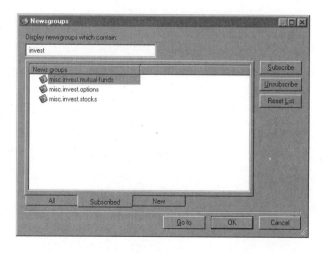

Newsgroup acronyms

Here are some of the acronyms used most frequently by newsgroup participants:

BTW	By the way
IMHO	In my humble opinion
OTOH	On the other hand
ROTFL	Rolling on the floor, laughing
RTFM	Read the *fill-in-the-blank* manual
WRT	With respect to
YMMV	Your mileage (experience) may vary

For demonstration purposes, we might as well show you how to unsubscribe from a newsgroup. Try this:

1. On the Subscribed tab of the Newsgroups dialog box, select the *misc.invest.options* newsgroup and then click the Unsubscribe button. Outlook Express accordingly removes the icon for this newsgroup from the list.

Unsubscribing from a newsgroup

2. Click OK to close the dialog box. In the Outlook Express window, the two subscribed newsgroups are now listed under your news settings.

Controlling the Display of Articles

Let's check out a few of the articles in the *misc.invest.-mutual-funds* newsgroup:

1. Click *misc.invest.mutual-funds* in the left pane. Outlook Express downloads the newsgroup's articles and displays their headers in the top right pane.

2. Click the first header to display its article in the preview pane, as shown here:

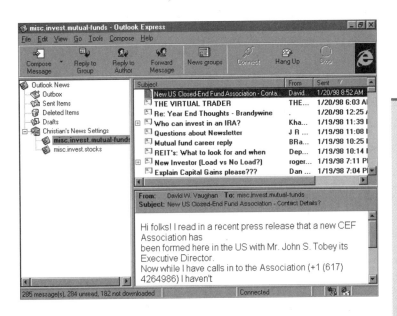

Checking the numbers

If you click your news settings entry in the left pane, Outlook Express displays in the right pane a list of subscribed newsgroups with the total number of articles and the number you have not read. From this information you can judge whether to display a newsgroup's articles. If you keep up with the articles in a subscribed newsgroup, you can tell whether anything new has been posted since your last visit just by looking at this list.

Outlook Express indicates that the article has been read by changing its header's type. The number of articles listed, the number of unread articles, and the number available but not yet downloaded are displayed in the Outlook Express status bar at the bottom of the screen.

Threads and follow-ups

3. Scroll through the list in the top pane, clicking the headers of any articles of interest. Notice that articles are organized into clusters, called *threads*, that consist of the original article and any responses, called *follow-ups*. So instead of reading newsgroups chronologically, you read subject-based threads that may have evolved over several days or even weeks as various people added their two cents.

By default, Outlook Express downloads and displays the headers of the 300 newest articles. Suppose we have read these messages and we now want to see others that we haven't read. Here's what we do:

Hiding read articles

1. Click the headers of a dozen or so articles that don't have plus signs beside them, pausing long enough on each one for it to change from bold to regular type.

2. Choose Current View and then Unread Messages from the View menu.

3. Now scroll the list of articles, noticing that all those you clicked in step 1 have disappeared from the list.

4. Repeat step 1 for the next several *misc.invest.mutual-funds* articles.

5. Now click *misc.invest.stocks* in the left pane and then click *misc.invest.mutual-funds* again (this gives it a chance to update its contents to reflect the changes you have made). The headers for the articles you clicked in step 4 have disappeared from the top right pane.

6. To retrieve more articles, choose Download This Newsgroup from the Tools menu to display this dialog box:

Getting a handle on large newsgroups

When you first start reading a newsgroup, the number of articles can seem overwhelming. To start with, you might want to mark all the articles as read by choosing the Mark All As Read command from the Edit menu. Then you can read all new articles posted from today on, without feeling compelled to go back and read existing articles. (Usenet wisdom has it that anything worth discussing will come up again, and you can catch it next time around.)

7. Select the Get The Following Items check box, ensure that New Headers is selected, and then click OK. Outlook Express then downloads the headers for the remaining articles in the *misc.invest.mutual-funds* newsgroup.

As you scrolled through the list of *misc.invest.mutual-funds* articles, you probably noticed all the threads indicated by plus signs. Let's read a thread:

1. Click the plus sign preceding a thread that does not begin with *Re:*, such as the one shown here:

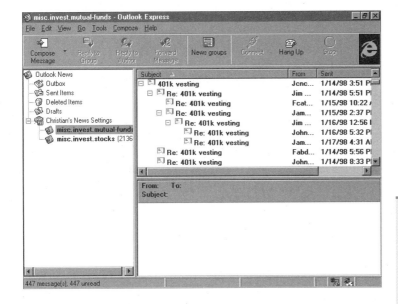

The *Re:* in the headers of the indented articles indicates that they are follow-ups to the top-level article.

Reading a thread

Downloading more articles

Outlook Express can retrieve a maximum of 1000 articles at a time. When you display a newsgroup, by default the program retrieves about 300 articles. To increase this number, choose Options from the Tools menu and on the Read tab, change the setting in the Download box. Alternatively, you can choose Get Next 300 Headers from the Tools menu to see 300 new articles at a time.

2. Click the plus sign preceding the header of a thread that does begin with *Re:*, and then select the top-level header. The *Re:* indicates that this article and those that are indented under it are responses to an earlier article that is no longer part of the thread because it has expired (see page 147).

3. Click one of the lower-level articles in the thread to display it in the preview pane.

Marking a thread as read

4. You've read enough of this thread to know that it's of no interest to you, so choose Mark Thread As Read from the Edit menu. The entire thread is marked as read, even though you displayed only a couple of its articles.

Suppose we have read all the articles and we want to follow up on some of them, so we don't want "read" articles to be removed if we switch to another group. Follow these steps:

Displaying all articles

1. Choose Current View and then All Messages from the View menu and press Ctrl+Home to move to the first header in the top right pane. The headers of all the read articles reappear.

Marking a newsgroup as read

2. Choose Mark All As Read from the Edit menu to mark the entire newsgroup as read.

OK, so now all the messages are displayed and they are all marked as read. But how do you identify those you want to follow up on? You can mark them as unread so that only they appear in the list in bold type, and you can then jump from unread message to unread message. Try this:

Other ways of sorting

As you'll see if you choose Sort By from the View menu, articles are grouped by thread (so that the articles that belong to a thread appear together no matter when they were sent) and then by the date they were sent. You won't want to change the Group Messages By Thread setting, but you might want to sort the articles by subject or by sender. Experiment with different sort orders to see which work best for you.

1. First, choose Sort By from the View menu and check that Sent is selected and Ascending is deselected on the submenu so that the most recent articles appear first in the top right pane.

2. Click a header to display its article in the preview pane.

3. Choose Mark As Unread from the Edit menu.

4. Repeat steps 2 and 3 to mark a few more articles as unread.

5. Now press Ctrl+Home to move to the top of the list, and choose Next and then Next Unread Message from the View menu to jump to the first "unread" article.

6. Press Ctrl+U to jump to the second unread article.

7. With the article displayed in the preview pane and without quitting Outlook Express, disconnect from your ISP by clicking the Hang Up button.

Having read a few articles contributed by others, let's see how you might contribute some of your own.

Following Up on Articles

Suppose we want to follow up on the article whose text is now displayed in the preview pane. Follow these steps:

1. Click the Reply To Group button on the toolbar to display this window:

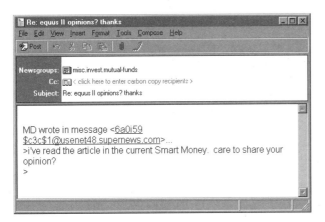

Notice that the Newsgroups and Subject boxes are already filled in. The subject is the same as that of the article you are following up on, with *Re:* added if the original article is the start of a thread. If this article has already been stored on your hard drive, or if you are connected to your ISP, the original article appears at the bottom of the message area preceded by > marks. You can edit this quoted material as appropriate.

Moving among unread articles

The Hang Up button

The Reply To Group button

Efficient browsing

To browse a newsgroup's headers offline, right-click the newsgroup in the left pane and choose Properties from the object menu. On the Download tab, click the When Downloading check box, select New Headers, and click OK. Offline, you can browse through the headers, select an article, and choose Mark For Retrieval and Mark Message from the Tools menu. Then connect to your ISP and choose Download All from the Tools menu to get the full text of the marked articles. To browse and mark headers online, choose Options from the Tools menu, click the Read tab, deselect the Automatically Show News Messages In The Preview Pane check box and click OK. To read an article, select its header and then press the Spacebar.

Sending via Outbox

2. For demonstration purposes, type a short, courteous reply and choose Send Later from the File menu. Depending on the length of the article and of your reply, you might see this dialog box:

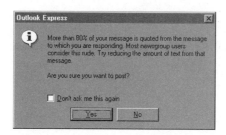

3. In this case, you can simply click Yes. Then click OK in the Post News Message box.

The Post button

That's it! Under normal circumstances, we would be connected to our ISP and could click the Post button on the toolbar to send the follow-up on its way. As it is, Outlook Express puts the follow-up in Outbox, waiting for the next time we connect to the Internet.

Bear in mind that sometimes it is more appropriate to e-mail a response to the person who posted an article than it is to take up the time of newsgroup members with a follow-up, especially if the response contributes little to the general discussion. (A *thank you* note falls into this category.) To do this, you can simply click the Reply To Author button to send an e-mail response. You can also click the Forward Message button to forward a copy of an article via e-mail to a specific person.

The Reply To Author and Forward Message buttons

Posting New Articles

Composing and posting new articles is very similar to composing and sending e-mail messages except that we don't have to enter the address of the recipient. Follow these steps to try it now:

1. With the *misc.invest.mutual-funds* newsgroup still active in the left pane of the Outlook Express window, click the

Compose Message button to open a window with the newsgroup's name already in the Newsgroups box.

The Compose Message button

2. Type a subject, press Tab, and type an article like this one:

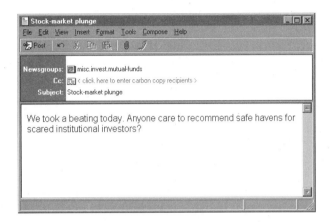

3. Because you are not connected to your ISP, choose Send
   Later from the File menu to simulate posting the article.

4. When a message appears telling you the article will be placed
   in your Outbox, click OK.

   If we were actually posting this article, it would show up in
   the newsgroup after a while as the beginning of a new thread.
   Other people's follow-ups would be given *Re:* headers and be
   grouped under our article to designate them as responses,
   whether they were posted hours or even days later.

   We have one bit of tidying up to do before we end this section.
   We used the Send Later command, so our articles are now sitting in Outlook Express's Outbox and we need to delete them:

1. Click Outbox in the left pane of the Outlook Express window
   to display its two items in the top right pane.

2. Select both articles and click the Delete button on the toolbar.
   Now there's no chance that your bogus articles will waste the
   time of the *misc.invest.mutual-funds* members.

3. Close Outlook Express.

Newsgroup Etiquette

The procedure for posting articles to a newsgroup is relatively simple. The etiquette involved can be another matter, depending on the nature of the newsgroup we want to post in. Some newsgroups are inherently inflammatory and nothing we can say will turn up the heat any higher. Others are informal and are much more forgiving of the mistakes *newbies* (new users) can make. But the most informative and useful newsgroups are often those that have been around for a while and whose participants get irritated when newcomers barge in without bothering to learn their rules. These rules are perfectly reasonable and are designed to avoid wasting everyone's time, so bear them in mind:

- **Read the newsgroup's FAQ.** For Usenet newsgroups, look in *news.answers* or in the category's *.answers* newsgroup. The FAQs are required reading for anyone wanting to post an article to some newsgroups. Take these requirements seriously if you want to be taken seriously by the group.

- **Read all the newsgroup's existing articles.** And we mean *all* the articles. This gives you a feel for the kinds of issues the newsgroup deals with. If you're burning to ask a question or to bring up an issue that doesn't fit the pattern, look somewhere else. Off-topic articles can provoke strident follow-ups. Also make sure someone hasn't already asked your question or put your issue on the table for discussion.

The main point to remember is that every article we post takes up time for the newsgroup's readers and takes up disk space on the thousands of news servers that are the backbone of the newsgroup system. Tossing a casual contribution into a newsgroup as we whiz by may seem harmless enough, but why bother if we don't intend to return to see people's responses? The value of a newsgroup depends on the quality of the ideas and information exchanged over time or on the fun people have communicating electronically with each other. If you spend much time in a newsgroup, you'll find that you get out of it only as much as you put into it, and pretty soon, you'll get as irritated by casual intruders as the veteran members do.

Advertising

Commercial advertising is really frowned on in most newsgroups and is likely to instigate strident follow-ups (as well as boycotts). *Spamming* (the practice of posting the same material to multiple newsgroups) is virulently opposed, not only by newsgroup members themselves but also by ISPs, who have been known to cancel the accounts of people caught in the act. Some newsgroups tolerate a simple, non-hyped announcement of a new product or service that directly relates to the members' interests. Such announcements are less likely to raise hackles if they come from a seasoned member with a reputation for intelligent participation in the newsgroup; in other words, don't just drop in on a newsgroup and make an announcement. Some categories have want-ad or marketplace subcategories for personal, not commercial, transactions. The usefulness of these newsgroups is limited, however, because not many people will buy used merchandise without seeing and testing it.

Communicating with NetMeeting

Internet Explorer comes with NetMeeting, which supplements the written communication provided by Outlook with some exciting direct communication capabilities. With Net-Meeting, we can collaborate with others by working on documents that we can all see and edit on our screens. We can also work on graphics using a whiteboard visible to all parties. We can chat with other people by each typing what we want to say in a shared window. And we can send and receive files. Net-Meeting also breaks new Internet ground in the realm of spoken and visual communications. If our computer is equipped with a sound card and a microphone, we can hold audioconferences instead of placing long-distance telephone calls; and if our computer is equipped with a video camera and a video capture card, we can hold videoconferences. In this section, we'll briefly describe NetMeeting so that you can decide whether you want to take advantage of its capabilities.

Before we can use NetMeeting, we need to set it up. Follow these steps:

1. Choose Internet Call and then Internet Call (again) from the Outlook Go menu. The NetMeeting Setup Wizard starts and displays its introductory dialog box.

   Setting up NetMeeting

2. Click Next, and then click Next again to accept the default directory server, *ils.microsoft.com*. (By the way, *ils* stands for *Internet locator server*.)

3. In the next dialog box, enter your e-mail address and fill in any other boxes you wish. (This information appears in the directory listing, so think twice before divulging personal information.) Then click Next.

4. Select a category of use—for example, we selected For Business Use—and click Next.

5. You may be asked to specifiy your connection speed. Make a selection and click Next.

6. The next step is to tune your audio settings by checking your voice. Follow the directions and when you are done, click

Finish. (If you don't have sound equipment on your computer, or if you want to communicate with text only, follow the wizard's instructions and click Finish just as you would if you did have a sound card and a microphone.)

7. If necessary, connect to your ISP.

8. If you see a message box that looks like this:

click OK and see the adjacent tip. You then see a NetMeeting window like this one (we've maximized it):

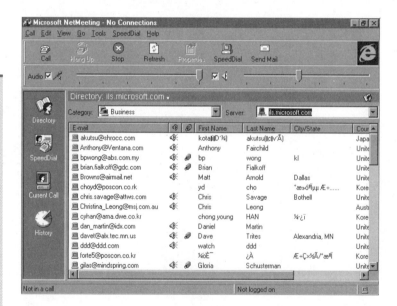

Problems connecting to a directory server

Sometimes when you log on to NetMeeting, you might see a message box telling you of some sort of problem connecting to the default server. You can try to access a different server by clicking the arrow at the right end of the Server box on the Directory tab and selecting an option from the drop-down list. When you locate an available server, you can designate it as the one you want to log on to by choosing Options from the Tools menu, clicking the Calling tab, selecting the server from the Server Name drop-down list, and clicking OK. NetMeeting then attempts to log you on to that server. The new Server Name setting remains in effect as the default until you change it again.

Notice that the viewing area of this window has a bar on the left side similar to the Outlook bar. At the moment, we are looking at the Directory view, which tells us the category of NetMeeting use, the directory server we are logged on to, and a good deal of information about all the other people who are also logged on to this particular directory.

9. To get ready for the next section, close NetMeeting and disconnect from your ISP.

Setting Up a Call

All NetMeeting activities take place in the context of a *call*. We first set up the call to establish contact with the person we want to communicate with and then indicate the type of communication we are going to use. As an example, suppose we want to "talk" to a colleague using NetMeeting. Here's how we would set up the call:

1. E-mail or phone the colleague and arrange for a NetMeeting call at a specific time and on a specific directory server. For this example, we have agreed to use *ils.business.four11.com* to talk.

← Agreeing on a time and place

2. At the designated time, start NetMeeting by choosing Internet Call and then Internet Call from the Go menu, and if necessary connect to your ISP.

3. Choose Options from the Tools menu, click the Calling tab, change the Server Name setting to *ils.business.four11.com*, and click OK. After a pause, the list on the Directory tab refreshes itself to display information about the other people logged on. Anybody with a computer icon designated by a red asterisk is already involved in a call. A file transfer icon indicates the person is either using Chat or the Whiteboard, collaborating on a project, or sending files. A speaker icon indicates that the person's computer has sound equipment, and a camera icon indicates that his or her computer has video equipment.

← Changing the directory server

4. Find the e-mail address of your colleague in the E-Mail column, right-click the listing, and choose Call from the object menu. The NetMeeting program on your computer contacts the NetMeeting program on your colleague's computer, asking whether he or she will accept the call. (This may take a while.) Once the call is accepted, the Current Call view of the NetMeeting window becomes active and lists the call participants, as shown on the following page.

Receiving calls

By default, when someone asks whether you want to participate in a call, NetMeeting displays a dialog box with the name of the caller and gives you the option of accepting or rejecting the call. You can tell NetMeeting to automatically accept calls by choosing Options from the Tools menu and selecting the Automatically Accept Incoming Calls option on the General tab. You can tell NetMeeting you don't want to be bothered by any calls by choosing the Do Not Disturb command from the Call menu.

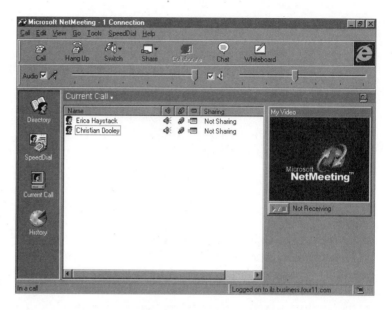

We can now communicate with call participants in a variety of ways, some of which we'll briefly discuss in the next few sections. When we are ready to end the call, we simply click the Hang Up button on the NetMeeting toolbar.

Chatting

Chatting is a relatively low-tech way of communicating by typing on the screen. It is popular because it's immediate, it's inexpensive, and unlike audio- and videoconferencing, more than two people can get involved in the conversation. (Social chatting also offers the advantage of being egalitarian: a user name does not necessarily specify age, race, gender, or able-bodied status, and people are required to respond only to the merits of each other's contributions. It is also anonymous: we can project a fantasy persona into cyberspace with very little risk that someone will call our bluff. Of course, the downside is that we never know whether the people we are "talking" to are also play-acting. The moral for those of you who want to use NetMeeting for socializing: have fun but be wary.) Assuming that you want to chat with the colleague with whom you've just established a call, follow these steps:

The Chat button

1. From the Current Call view of the NetMeeting window, click the Chat button on the toolbar to display the Chat window as shown on the facing page.

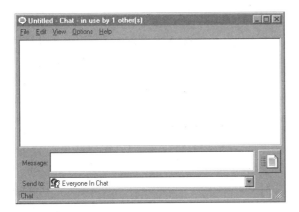

Clicking the Chat button automatically opens the Chat window on your colleague's screen as well as yours.

2. Type *When do you think you will be finished with your review of the new specifications?* and press Enter. The message appears both on your screen and your colleague's. Here's what our screen looks like after a keyboard conversation:

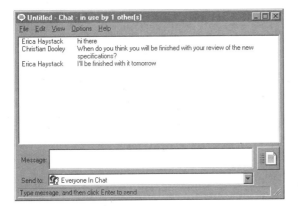

3. Click the Chat window's Close button to end the session, and when NetMeeting gives you the opportunity to save the conversation, click No.

We can save the conversation from a chat session at any time by choosing Save As from the File menu and assigning the chat file a name. Thereafter, we can save new versions of the same chat file by choosing the Save command. And we can print the conversation by choosing Print from the File menu.

Whispering

Suppose you are participating in a call with several other people and you want to chat with only one of them. You can select that person's name from the Send To drop-down list at the bottom of the Chat window, and when you type a message and press Enter, only that person will see what you typed.

Using the Whiteboard

Two or more call participants can work concurrently on graphic projects by using NetMeeting's Whiteboard component. The Whiteboard is an onscreen drawing board, where we can collaboratively diagram processes, work out schedules, sketch designs, and so on. For this example, suppose we want to come to an agreement with colleagues based in distant cities about the company reporting procedure. We have already established a NetMeeting call and now we want to use the Whiteboard to diagram the procedure. Follow these steps:

The Whiteboard button

1. Click the Whiteboard button on the toolbar to display the window shown here:

The Whiteboard automatically opens on the screens of all call participants when you send Whiteboard data to them. You can then capture parts of screens and place them on the Whiteboard using the commands at the bottom of the Tools menu; or you can copy items from other programs and paste them in from the Clipboard; or you can draw them from scratch.

The Unfilled Ellipse tool

2. Maximize the window, click the Unfilled Ellipse tool in the toolbox on the left side of the window, move to the top left corner of the window, hold down the left mouse button, and drag to draw a skinny oval.

The Text tool

3. Click the Text tool, click an insertion point at the left end of the oval, and type *Write* and your initials.

4. Continue to draw ovals and lines (using the Line tool) to create a diagram that looks something like this:

The Line tool

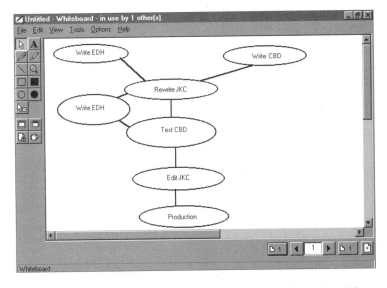

You can zoom in or out by choosing Zoom from the View menu or by clicking the Zoom button.

The Zoom button

5. When you've finished, save the contents of the Whiteboard by choosing the Save As command from the File menu and assigning a filename.

6. Close the Whiteboard window.

We can also print out a paper copy of the Whiteboard's contents by choosing Print from the File menu.

Sending and Receiving Files

Additionally, we can use NetMeeting's file sharing feature to send and receive files. Suppose that before terminating the call we decide that all the call participants should have a copy of the last annual report we wrote for Terra Firm. Here's how we would send the file to everyone:

1. Choose File Transfer and then Send File from the Tools menu to display the dialog box shown on the following page.

SpeedDial

By default, NetMeeting adds the people you call and who call you to a list on the SpeedDial tab of its window. Click a name in the SpeedDial list to request a call with that person. To send your SpeedDial information, click the SpeedDial button on Net-Meeting's toolbar, fill in the boxes, click Send To Mail Recipient, and click OK. (You can use this dialog box to manually add new SpeedDial information.) In the New Message window, enter the recipient's address and a Subject, and then send the message. Once your information is in their SpeedDial list, they can simply click it to contact you.

Collaborating on documents

You and your colleagues can collaborate on a document at two levels: View Only and Change. In View Only mode, the owner of the document shares it with call participants in such a way that they can see the document but cannot work on it. In Change mode, the owner gives other call participants full editing access to the document. First, choose Host Meeting from the Call menu. As other participants join your meeting, their names appear in Current Call view in everyone else's NetMeeting window. Then open the document on your computer, switch to NetMeeting, click the Share button on the NetMeeting toolbar, and switch back to the document to work on it. The document appears in a window on the participants' screens. To allow them to make changes, switch back to NetMeeting, click the Collaborate button on the NetMeeting toolbar, and flip back to the document. Any participant who wants to collaborate also clicks the Collaborate button. He or she can then click the mouse to take control of the cursor, and can insert and delete text in the usual way. (Obviously, only one person can edit the document at a time.) To regain control of the document and stop the collaboration, press Esc (or click the Collaborate button again to deselect it). To end the meeting, click the Hang Up button on the NetMeeting toolbar.

2. Navigate to the file you want to send, select it, and click Open. (You can also drag the file onto the list of people on the Current Call tab.) The NetMeeting status bar indicates the progress of the file transfer.

3. When you see a message telling you the transfer was completed successfully, click OK.

If we are on the receiving end of a file transfer, we see this dialog box when the transfer is complete:

We can then make a note of the name of the file and click Close. It will then be stored in the C:\Program Files\NetMeeting\Received Files folder.

Audioconferencing and Videoconferencing

Provided we have the necessary audio equipment, we can start a NetMeeting call and then carry on a conversation with one other audio-equipped participant by talking into a microphone and listening to responses over our speakers. And if we have the necessary video equipment, we can send and receive video images. Put the two together, and we can hold videoconferences. (The success of this experience depends a lot on our equipment and directory server traffic.) Here's how we might participate in an audioconference or videoconference with a colleague:

1. Assuming you have both started NetMeeting and are logged on to the same directory server, locate the e-mail address of your colleague and request a call.

2. When the call is accepted, make sure that check marks appear in the microphone and speaker check boxes on the Audio toolbar, and then test the volume of your microphone and speakers by exchanging a few words of greeting. Make any necessary adjustments using the two volume control bars. (You can mute the microphone or the speakers by deselecting their check boxes.)

   ← **Conversing over the Internet**

3. Say what you need to say.

4. End the audio session (but not the call) by clicking the speaker icon next to the name of the person you are talking to in Current Call view and choosing Stop Using Audio And Video from the object menu.

5. Finally, end the call by clicking the Hang Up button on the NetMeeting toolbar.

What about video? We can send video images to a call participant who does not have video equipment attached to his or her computer, and we can also receive images whether or not we have video equipment. However, assuming that both computers have the necessary cameras and video capture boards, follow the steps on the next page for videoconferencing.

Sending to one person

To send a file to only one of several call participants, right-click that person's name in Current Call view and choose Send File from the object menu. Then in the Open File dialog box, locate and double-click the file to start the transfer.

1. Before you set up a call, choose Options from the Tools menu and click the Video tab to display these options:

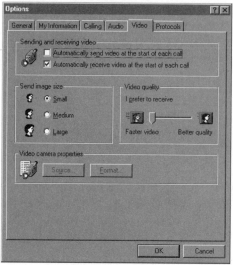

2. Select both the Automatically Send Video and Automatically Receive Video check boxes and click OK.

Sending video images ———▶ 3. Back in Directory view, locate the e-mail address of the colleague with whom you want to exchange video data and request a call. Assuming that both of you have selected the Automatically Receive Video and Automatically Send Video check boxes, you can now see the call participant (or whatever images he or she is sending you) in the Remote Video window in Current Call view.

What do you look like?

If you want to check before you establish the call what you will look like to the person receiving your video image, click the button at the bottom of the My Video window. Check the lighting, your position in relation to the camera, and so on. When you're satisfied, place the call and proceed with your videoconference.

Video on demand

To control when you send and receive video, you can deselect the Automatically Send Video and the Automatically Receive Video check boxes on the Video tab of the Options dialog box and then click the buttons at the bottom of the My Video and Remote Video windows to initiate the sending and receiving of video images.

4. When you've finished, end the video session by clicking the camera icon next to the name of the person you are communicating with in Current Call view and choosing Stop Using Audio And Video from the object menu.

5. Once again, end the call by clicking the Hang Up button on the NetMeeting toolbar.

You can start a call with several people and then talk to each of them in turn, or send video images to each in turn. Click the Switch button on the toolbar, select the name of the first person you want to communicate with, and talk and/or send video. Then click the Switch button, click the name of the second person, and talk and/or send video. And so on. While you are talking or sending video to one call participant, two other call participants can also be talking or sending video.

The Switch button

This has been a very quick overview of NetMeeting's capabilities—nothing more than a teaser, really. But if you frequently need to communicate with distant colleagues more directly than you can with e-mail (or regular mail), you might want to explore NetMeeting's capabilities further.

Congratulations! You have completed your Quick Course in Outlook. By now, you should feel comfortable with all the components of this program as well as other communications features accessible through Outlook. With the basics you have learned in this book, together with the Help feature, you should have no trouble creating any Outlook item and keeping it organized the way you want. Good luck!

Index

Keep things running smoothly around the Office.

These are *the* answer books for business users of Microsoft Office 97 applications. They are packed with everything from quick, clear instructions for new users to comprehensive answers for power users. The Microsoft Press® *Running* series features authoritative handbooks you'll keep by your computer and use every day.

Running Microsoft® Excel 97
Mark Dodge, Chris Kinata, and Craig Stinson
U.S.A. $39.95   ($54.95 Canada)
ISBN 1-57231-321-8

Running Microsoft® Word 97
Russell Borland
U.S.A. $39.95   ($53.95 Canada)
ISBN 1-57231-320-X

Running Microsoft® PowerPoint® 97
Stephen W. Sagman
U.S.A. $29.95   ($39.95 Canada)
ISBN 1-57231-324-2

Running Microsoft® Access 97
John L. Viescas
U.S.A. $39.95   ($54.95 Canada)
ISBN 1-57231-323-4

Running Microsoft® Office 97
Michael Halvorson and Michael Young
U.S.A. $39.95   ($53.95 Canada)
ISBN 1-57231-322-6

Microsoft Press

Take productivity in stride.

Microsoft Press® *Step by Step* books provide quick and easy self-paced training that will help you learn to use the powerful word processor, spreadsheet, database, desktop information manager, and presentation applications of Microsoft Office 97, both individually and together. Prepared by the professional trainers at Catapult, Inc., and Perspection, Inc., these books present easy-to-follow lessons with clear objectives, real-world business examples, and numerous screen shots and illustrations. Each book contains approximately eight hours of instruction. Put Microsoft's Office 97 applications to work today, *Step by Step*.

Microsoft *Press*

Things are looking up!

Here's the remarkable, *visual* way to quickly find answers about Microsoft applications and operating systems. Microsoft Press® *At a Glance* books let you focus on particular tasks and show you with clear, numbered steps the easiest way to get them done right now.

Microsoft® Excel 97 At a Glance
Perspection, Inc.
U.S.A. $16.95   ($22.95 Canada)
ISBN 1-57231-367-6

Microsoft® Word 97 At a Glance
Jerry Joyce and Marianne Moon
U.S.A. $16.95   ($22.95 Canada)
ISBN 1-57231-366-8

Microsoft® PowerPoint® 97 At a Glance
Perspection, Inc.
U.S.A. $16.95   ($22.95 Canada)
ISBN 1-57231-368-4

Microsoft® Access 97 At a Glance
Perspection, Inc.
U.S.A. $16.95   ($22.95 Canada)
ISBN 1-57231-369-2

Microsoft® Office 97 At a Glance
Perspection, Inc.
U.S.A. $16.95   ($22.95 Canada)
ISBN 1-57231-365-X

Microsoft® Windows® 95 At a Glance
Jerry Joyce and Marianne Moon
U.S.A. $16.95   ($22.95 Canada)
ISBN 1-57231-370-6

Microsoft®*Press*

Get quick, easy answers— anywhere!

Microsoft® Excel 97 Field Guide
Stephen L. Nelson
U.S.A. $9.95 ($12.95 Canada)
ISBN 1-57231-326-9

Microsoft® Word 97 Field Guide
Stephen L. Nelson
U.S.A. $9.95 ($12.95 Canada)
ISBN 1-57231-325-0

Microsoft® PowerPoint® 97 Field Guide
Stephen L. Nelson
U.S.A. $9.95 ($12.95 Canada)
ISBN 1-57231-327-7

Microsoft® Outlook™ 97 Field Guide
Stephen L. Nelson
U.S.A. $9.99 ($12.99 Canada)
ISBN 1-57231-383-8

Microsoft® Access 97 Field Guide
Stephen L. Nelson
U.S.A. $9.95 ($12.95 Canada)
ISBN 1-57231-328-5

Microsoft Press® Field Guides are a quick, accurate source of information about Microsoft Office 97 applications. In no time, you'll have the lay of the land, identify toolbar buttons and commands, stay safely out of danger, and have all the tools you need for survival!

Microsoft Press® products are available worldwide wherever quality computer books are sold. For more information, contact your book or computer retailer, software reseller, or local Microsoft Sales Office, or visit our Web site at mspress.microsoft.com. To locate your nearest source for Microsoft Press products, or to order directly, call 1-800-MSPRESS in the U.S. (in Canada, call 1-800-268-2222).

Prices and availability dates are subject to change.

***Microsoft**·Press*

Register Today!

Return this
Quick Course® in Microsoft® Outlook™ 98
registration card for
a Microsoft Press® catalog

U.S. and Canada addresses only. Fill in information below and mail postage-free. Please mail only the bottom half of this page.

1-57231-846-5   *QUICK COURSE® IN*   *Owner Registration Card*
MICROSOFT® OUTLOOK™ 98

NAME

INSTITUTION OR COMPANY NAME

ADDRESS

CITY   STATE   ZIP

Microsoft®*Press*
Quality Computer Books

**For a free catalog of
Microsoft Press® products, call
1-800-MSPRESS**